THE
VICTORIANS
at CHRISTMAS

The Transformation of Tradition

David Parker

HALSGROVE

DEDICATION

This book is dedicated to Pamela, my wife, in gratitude for making so many Christmases so very enjoyable.

ACKNOWLEDGEMENTS

It is with pleasure that I acknowledge the generosity of the trustees, director (Emma Dunn) and librarian (Sonia Llewellyn) of the Devon & Exeter Institution in Exeter's Cathedral Close in granting me regular access to its carefully conserved volumes of the *Illustrated London News* and permission to photograph the images used in this book. And I remain very grateful to Mark Ware MFA for his time and expert professional skills in reproducing and refining those images for me.

First published in Great Britain in 2023

British Library Cataloguing-in-Publication Data
A CIP record for this title is available from the British Library

ISBN 978 0 85704 368 9

Halsgrove Publishing
Halsgrove House,
Ryelands Business Park,
Bagley Road, Wellington, Somerset TA21 9PZ
Tel: 01823 653777
Fax: 01823 216796
email: sales@halsgrove.com

Part of the Halsgrove group of companies
Information on all Halsgrove titles is available at: www.halsgrove.com

Printed and bound in India by Parksons Graphics Ltd

Opposite: John Leech: Going to the pantomime – ILN 24 December 1853.

Contents

Henry Stephen (Hal) Ludlow (1861-c1934): Ali Baba & the Forty Thieves – ILN 1 January 1887.

CHAPTER 1

Introduction:
Sources and Interpretations

The influential, if controversial, philosopher Jacques Derrida (1930-2004) argued that as soon as writers and artists complete a work its meaning is open to differing interpretations. His term 'difference' refers to his point that meaning cannot be regarded as fixed or static, but is always evolving. Indeed any meaning may be what a writer or artist intended, but it might well be something else arrived at by someone else reading and observing the work. This process of personal questioning and arriving at tentative conclusions gained the name 'deconstruction'. Derrida accepted that uncertainty might lie at the centre of the process, but he highlighted that 'deconstruction' takes place everywhere, whether consciously or not, and is an inevitable and important part of our search for understanding. All this is particularly relevant to this book which explores the evolution of the celebration of Christmas during the reign of Queen Victoria through contemporary illustrations and commentaries. It seeks to 'deconstruct' them and thereby, however tenuously, arrive at an understanding of what Christmas meant to the Victorians, and how their expression and experience of this increasing popular festival reflected their wider attitudes, aspirations and anxieties.

The book uses the illustrations and accompanying articles from the celebrated *Illustrated London News.* It concentrates upon the half a century from 1842 to 1892, a period when modern machinery enabled engravings to be reproduced clearly, rapidly and cheaply, and before photographs found their initially fuzzy way into journals and newspapers and ousted older techniques. Founded in 1842 by Herbert Ingram, a Nottingham printer and newsagent, the pioneering *Illustrated London News (ILN)* sought to do exactly what its title proclaimed – illustrate the latest news, and with a dynamic and clarity unknown before. In May that year its first edition proudly proclaimed it would create an invaluable archive that would provide *mile-stones upon the travelled road of time* that would otherwise have been lost. Its host of skilled, and often well-known, artists and engravers set to work to produce a steady stream of pictures based upon their personal observation of people and events, or the notes and drawings of others at the scene, or indeed just their imaginative and often dramatic interpretation of what had happened. It prided itself though, with justification, that its staff travelled far and wide across the country, and the world, to secure at first hand the latest news and images. The *ILN* was as interested in the achievements of Science and the Arts as it was in the ups and downs of successive governments, international crises and the waging of major wars. And as Christmas grew to become a major festival in Victorian lives, so it filled more and more pages in the *ILN's* late December editions until a lavishly illustrated special Christmas Supplement became a standard annual issue.

Overall the *ILN* treated its readers as well-educated and serious minded, and was moderately Liberal rather than Conservative in outlook. Herbert Ingram was a progressive Liberal MP for Boston from 1856 until his death in 1860 – from drowning after a pleasure boat collision on Lake Michigan in North America. A son, William, another Liberal MP, took over the paper. The *ILN* eschewed sensationalism, and within its Liberal bias it sought balance in its reports of conflicts and controversies. It had little sympathy with violent strikes, but ensured its readers were fully aware of working class aspirations and the plight of the poor, and handled the frequent protest movements, and notably Chartism, with consistent even-handedness. It was forward looking, and highlighted technological advances, but also noted the price paid in terms of the social dislocation caused by the decline of older ways of working, rural depopulation and the largely uncontrolled spread of smoke-ridden towns. It had a particular hatred of the mean-spirited Poor Law Amendment Act of 1834 and the degrading workhouses built in its wake.

Not surprisingly it delighted in royal events, aristocratic weddings and funerals, the splendours of great estates, and visits by overseas ruling families. However it also entertained readers with cartoons mocking events such as the Derby, the Henley Regatta, outings to the seaside, and the hunt. There were some provocative tongue-in-cheek articles, and sometimes what appeared to be sentimental texts and poems took unexpected and thought provoking turns – and examples of these appear later in the book. The *ILN* soared in popularity, with weekly sales rising from 26,000 copies at 6d each in 1842 to 65,000 the following year, with intermittent peaks of 250,000 at the time of the Great Exhibition in 1851 and the Crimean War a few years later.

Generally speaking illustrations did not stand alone. In many cases the *ILN*'s artists were also its report writers, and notably so during the numerous overseas military campaigns and scientific expeditions. Sometimes, though, other authors compiled a report the *ILN*'s editor attached to a particular image and sometimes this story veered interestingly away from its nominal host. Images of battles were usually enshrined in lengthy reports of wider diplomatic activity. Pictures of life in British colonies were usually accompanied by lengthy discourses justifying British rule in terms of economic opportunities and peaceful development. And many Christmas illustrations had commentaries that steered the observer/reader into considering wider social and moral themes. It was as though, as Derrida argued, the article acts *by way of compensation for what ought to lack nothing at all in itself.* The text sometimes purports to tell us what it claims the illustration fail to show, or conversely the writer thinks the illustration might say too much without the article there to channel the readers' interpretation. There is from time to time a fascinating, and informative, dissonance between the two forms of representation. As we shall see, the *ILN* set out to use illustrations to bring both immediacy and intensity to its readers'

understanding of the world around them, and it used both the images and articles in diverse ways to suggest particular meaning and/or raise questions and issues.

Christmas was increasingly treated differently to other events as the decades passed. As the festival grew in intensity from the 1850s onwards, so festive-related images, stories and articles proliferated throughout the weeks straddling Christmas and New Year, and in the lavish Christmas Supplement. Many illustrations had seasonal poetry, of generally modest quality, linked to them. By the 1880s all of the late November and December editions included large eye-catching advertisements parading a vast array of goods now that the habit of giving presents to family, friends, servants and business acquaintances was well-established. And by the end of the decade the smiling rotund figure of Father Christmas had arrived from the United States of America and displaced the leering bucolic figure of 'Old Christmas' who disappeared back into the ancient forests from whence he came.

Some particularly evocative illustrations stood alone, with just a thought provoking and often slyly ambiguous title. The *ILN* thought they needed no elaboration, and, as will be seen, many incorporated a revealing, even tantalising, range of human hopes and fears during the heightened emotions of Christmas-time. Being so successful, the *ILN* numbered many artists among its contributors who were highly regarded (and many still so) and clearly capable of penetrating and capturing the human condition. It is safe to assume that many of the pictures were Victorian 'conversation pieces' which allowed and encouraged readers to ponder upon, and discuss, what might be happening and what people were thinking. Many Christmas illustrations centred upon major nineteenth century themes such as social class and attitudes to poverty, marriage, and the upbringing of children. Skilfully composed 'conversation pieces' raised many intriguing questions for the insightful observer.

The *ILN* was not averse to pinpointing the down-side of Christmas. In 1876 it printed a cartoon by Harry Furniss entitled *Christmas: Ideal & Real* which suggested that many people had a less than happy time, or at least a mix of experiences. Pristine snow could turn to dangerous slush, ice could prove perilously thin, carol singers (the

Harry Furniss: Christmas, Ideal and Real – ILN 1876 Christmas Supplement.

historic 'waits') could be threatening rather than joyous, invitations to stand under the mistletoe were not always enticing, households could be plagued by seekers after Christmas Boxes, and the cost of Christmas with all the trimmings could easily prove worryingly high. Furniss suggests all this, and no doubt the generally middle-class readers of the *ILN* appreciated the points, but the artist is, perhaps, suggesting that a joyous Christmas is as much about personal attitudes as it is material circumstances. As Ebenezer Scrooge in *The Christmas Carol* exemplified, misery could be internally generated as much as externally imposed.

Stereotypically the Victorians were serious minded, but many contemporary illustrations poked fun at their pretensions. They were supposed to be deeply religious, but some illustrations see church going as a dull duty or as an opportunity to meet the opposite sex. Victorian women were believed to be tender-hearted and ultra-sensitive, but numerous illustrations reveal their pragmatic attitude towards killing live animals they kept or hunted. Women were supposed to be demure and restrained but pictures of dances and parties readily give the lie to such suggestions. A number of Christmas illustrations explore women's hopes at a time when marriage was the expected condition, but conversely a rising number of literary and artistic critics were portraying it as little more than imprisonment. The Victorians might have considered themselves beneficiaries of a new rational and technological age but they delighted in pantomimes featuring particularly grotesque and macabre characters and a marked degree of cruelty, and in stories where fairies, elves and sprites of uncertain temperaments could be alluring one minute and vivious the next. Maybe it was an example of cathartic Art mimicking perilous Life. And numerous pictures highlight the equivocal Victorian attitude towards the very poor whose plight touched the heartstrings but also reinforced the comforting notion that too much charity was unnecessary as the poor must be encouraged to better themselves rather than be softened in spirit by excessive handouts. The stigma that abject poverty was usually the result of morally reprehensible behaviour never went away, even at Christmas. The *ILN*'s Christmas editions were no doubt thought provoking to the Victorians as they strove to keep pace with their rapidly changing world, and they are no less revealing to us as we seek to understand our forebears and from whence we came.

It is often assumed that Charles Dickens invented the festive Christmas for the Victorians when *A Christmas Carol* was published on 19 December 1843. This is not a wholly accurate claim as we shall see, but the *ILN* was among those who immediately appreciated the book's appeal. Four days after its publication the *ILN* included vivid extracts in its summary of the spine-tingling story of a series of Spirits using scenes of past, present and future Christmases to transform the most grasping, selfish and miserable of human beings into someone capable of compassion, generosity and enjoyment. Dickens was saying there was something very special about Christmas. It made people people see others, and themselves, differently.

The story reflected life in early Victorian London, and the descriptions are evocative. It is three o'clock in the afternoon on Christmas Eve, it is *cold, bleak, biting weather. The fog is pouring in at every chink and keyhole,* and in the dismal court outside the money-lender Ebenezer Scrooge's door people *go wheezing up and down, beating their hand upon their breasts, and stamping their feet upon the pavement stones to warm them.* In the street water trickling from a pipe turned to *misanthropic ice,* and labourers repairing some gas pipes lit a great fire in a brazier around which ragged men and boys stealthily gather. In marked contrast *the brightness of the shops where holly sprigs and berries crackled in the lamp-heat of the windows made pale faces ruddy as they passed.* In *a dismal cell* inside Scrooge's office Bob Cratchit, his clerk, makes do with a fire *that looked like one coal.* Then Scrooge's nephew bursts in with Christmas greetings only to be rebuffed with the sneer *Bah! Humbug!* and a dismissal of a *Merry Christmas* as a waste of time and money, especially for weak-willed folk of inadequate means.

Meanwhile the fog and darkness thickened, so that people ran about with flaring links (torches of tarred waste fabric), *proffering their services to go before horses with carriages, and conduct them on their way.* A bell in nearby church tower invisible in the fog sombrely struck the hours and quarters, and *after his melancholy dinner in his usual melancholy tavern* Scrooge returned to his *gloomy suite of rooms in a lowering pile of buildings* that once belonged to his partner Jacob Marley, now dead and little missed.

That night Scrooge encounters four ghostly visitors. The first is Marley bound with chains entwined with *cash-boxes, keys, padlocks, ledgers, deeds and heady purses*, and now ruefully aware that despite priding himself as a 'good man of business' he is condemned for his greed and selfishness. He warns Scrooge to avoid a similar fate.

The Ghost of Christmas Past whisks Scrooge back decades to a Christmas Eve party arranged by Mr and Mrs Fezziwig for their family and employees, one of whom was the young Ebenezer. They were, of course, the antithesis of Scrooge and early on the young Belle had rejected Scrooge as her suitor as she was so disturbed by his obsession with money. As the party got under way *'in came a fiddler with a music book...... In came Mrs Fezziwig, one vast substantial smile. In came the three Miss Fezziwigs, beaming and lovable. In came the six young followers whose hearts they broke. In came all the young men and women employed in the business. In came the house-maid, with her cousin, the baker. In came the cook, with her brother's particular friend, the milkman.* They all danced, *and there were forfeits, and more dances, and there was cake, and there was negus* (a hot drink of port, lemon, sugar and spice), *and there was a great piece of cold roast, and there was a great piece of cold boiled, and there were mince pies, and plenty of beer.*

In fact the Ghost of Christmas Past was fortunate that the Fezziwigs held such a party, as in the early 1800s, when (it seems safe to assume) Scrooge was young, businesses such as the Fezziwigs where the owner's family lived among their workers in a mutually dependent social hierarchy were already on their way to becoming a rarity. Certainly by 1843 most Victorians saw Christmas festivities as essentially family occasions, with servants as necessary but socially separate celebrants, and any employees kept at a greater distance and left to their own devices. In the burgeoning Victorian industrial and commercial towns owners of businesses increasingly sought elegant houses well away from the sources of their wealth. The urban employers and their workers were increasingly ghettoed and if not exactly ignorant of each other they kept their distance.

The Spirit of Christmas Present is next. Amidst snow turned black by the smoke and soot, and furrowed by countless wagons, people were out on the streets. Dickens creates a mouth-watering scene for those who could afford it. *The poulterers' shops were still half open, and the fruiterers were radiant in their glory. There were great round pot-bellied baskets of chestnuts, shaped like the waistcoats of jolly old gentlemen, lolling at the doors, and tumbling out into the street in their apoplectic opulence. There were ruddy, brown-faced, broad-girthed Spanish Onions, shining in fatness of their growth like Spanish Friars, and winking from their shelves in wanton shyness at the girls as they went by, and glanced demurely at the hung-up mistletoe. There were pears and apples, clustered high in blooming pyramids; there were bunches of grapes, made in the shop-keepers' benevolence to dangle from conspicuous hooks, that people's mouths might water gratis as they passed; there were piles of filberts* (hazelnuts), *mossy and brown, recalling in their fragrance ancient walks among the woods, and pleasant shufflings ankle deep in withered leaves; there were Norfolk Biffins* (dark red apples) *squab and swarthy, setting off the yellow of the oranges and lemons, and in the great compactness of their juicy persons, earnestly beseeching and entreating to be taken home in paper bags, and eaten after dinner.'* The same was true of the grocers with the *blended scents of tea and coffee* assaulting the senses along with the boxes of raisins, almonds and spices, sticks of cinnamon, tempting *moisty and pulpy* figs, and the bowls of *candied fruits so caked and spotted with molton sugar.* In the 1840s Christmas was already a retailer's delight.

The Spirit shows Scrooge happy crowds thronging to churches and chapels, and poorer families joyfully taking their dinners (pieces of goose, mash potato and perhaps a little apple sauce) to be cooked in local bakers' ovens. It is a perfect day – *No fog, no mist, bright jovial, stirring cold; cold piping the blood to dance to; Golden sunlight; Heavenly sky; sweet fresh air; merry bells. Oh, glorious! Glorious!* The Spirit carries a miraculous torch from which he pours a blessing of incense on the dinners and a sprinkling of water onto those he saw quarrelling. *Their good humour was restored directly. For they said it was a shame to quarrel on Christmas Day. And so it was, God love it, so it was!* Taking Scrooge on a voyage of discovery, the *Spirit stood beside sick beds, and they were cheerful; on foreign lands and they were close at home; by struggling men, and they were greater in their patient hope; by poverty, and it was rich. In almshouses, hospitals, and gaol, in misery's every refuge, where vain man in his little brief authority had not made fast the door, and barred the Spirit out, he left his blessing, and taught Scrooge his precepts.*

Dickens deliberately left readers uncomfortable with the thought that such good cheer was not enough. Beneath the Spirit's long cloak peered two emaciated children. Called Ignorance and Want, they were *yellow, meagre, ragged, scowling and wolfish,* and stalked, shamed and threatened the land in their desperate need of compassion, resolution and eradication. They linked strongly with the final Spirit of Christmas Yet To Come who showed Scrooge a charwoman, laundress and an undertaker stealing a dead person's possessions to sell, a poor couple pleased that the person's death had freed them from debt, a few mourners who, far from mourning, were there for the free meal, and a neglected, forgotten, tombstone with the name Ebenezer Scrooge on it. Overcome, Scrooge promises to try to keep Christmas in his heart throughout the year – the true Christmas message. *The Spirits of all Three shall strive within me.* He starts by providing his impoverished clerk's family – the Cratchits – with Christmas dinner, paying Bob a living wage and caring for his crippled son, Tiny Tim. And then, full of Christmas cheer brought about by his new-found compassion, Scrooge is made welcome at his nephew's family gathering and Christmas dinner.

As the *Illustrated London News* immediately appreciated, *A Christmas Carol* seemed to encapsulate the heart and soul of an early Victorian Christmas. The family was at the heart of society and should be celebrated at Christmas, and conspicuous consumption was acceptable as it was the fruit of God's bounty, and those with means should express the compassionate Spirit of Christmas with acts of kindness to those with very little or nothing. The story was an exploration of the Incarnation and Atonement, and saw Scrooge liberated by God's grace which then led to his good works. It saw Christmas and its interwoven threads of spiritual reflection and material festivity as a salutary time in people's lives. And there was the disconcerting fact that the wraiths of Ignorance and Want would not stay hidden from open sight for long. Indeed, as readers of Dickens and the *ILN* knew only too well, their baleful presence was very well-known in 1843. Millions lived in poverty, and few received an education. Both were a condemnation of a Christian society failing in its duty, and both represented an ominous rising threat to that society.

CHAPTER 2

From Old Christmas to Father Christmas: The Transformation of Tradition

Customs From the Mists of Time

In Great Britain Christmas is a mid-winter festival with multiple attributes, including acts of worship celebrating the birth of Jesus, decorating a Christmas tree, wishing everyone seasonal joy, gathering with members of one's family, giving and receiving presents, and eating a special Christmas dinner. The full extent of the festivities owes much to the spread of Victorian middle class wealth and leisure, along with the growth of internal and external trade, the expansion of retail trade and consumerism, an efficient postal service and the increasing ease of railway travel. And as we have seen, Charles Dickens played an imaginative and significant role. However the roots of the fruitful celebration lay deep in the past.

Midwinter celebrations were common in distant centuries. Saturnalia was a lengthy Roman festival characterised by wild indulgence of every kind dedicated to the god Saturn during the winter solstice in December. The Romans also celebrated the Birthday of the Unconquered Sun (*Dies Natalis Solis Invicti*) on 25 December. The birthday of Mithras, called the Invincible Sun and worshipped by many soldiers, was on 25 December too – the date ordered by the Emperor Aurelian (270-275AD). In ancient Greece the god Dionoysis was identical to the Roman god Bacchus: both were gods of wine, and honoured with libidinous celebrations that lasted twelve days from 25 December, the gods' birthdays. For centuries tribes in Finland celebrated Beiwe, the sun-goddess of fertility during the winter solstice, and in the same season Russian communities marked the importance of the antlered goddess Rozhnitsa.

The Yule festival, common across much of northern Europe, occupied twelve mid-winter days, and was marked by, first, the honouring of the spirits of the dead, and then feasting and drinking accompanied by the wild behaviour eagerly anticipated on such occasions. In many communities there was the decorated Yule tree, and also the huge Yule log, dried from the previous year, that was burned with hopes that it would spark and crackle a great deal, and burn until the morning, to bring luck and prosperity to the household. The worship of trees was common among those with animistic beliefs in which natural objects possess spirits. In the Bible's *Second Book of Kings* the Hebrews who wandered away from the true God (*Yahweh*) decorated trees in groves near the altars of Baal. The Romans had sacred fig trees, and Germanic tribes honoured Wodin by tying fruits on evergreen trees. The holly plant was sacred to the Romans, and thought to bring good luck. The mistletoe was held to protect people near it from bad luck and make them more fertile – hence the kissing under it. The Yule goat represented the goats that pulled the God Thor's chariot across the sky. Across middle Europe he was known as Krampus, an evil spirit in horned goat form who roamed the world beating and even killing children who behaved badly. This terrifying beast found its way into Victorian children's stories, and featured in singularly disturbing Christmas cards. The beating of children by parents, nannies, teachers and employers, and threatening them with thoughts of divine or devilish retribution for misdemeanours, was a common adult Victorian pastime, as many elementary school logbooks, public school memoirs, autobiographies, children's storybooks and supposedly humorous poems record.

The Yule boar was the boar's head first presented to the god Freyr (of peace and fertility) and then eaten at the mid-winter feasting after being ceremonially paraded into the dining hall from

The arrival of the rustic masque and boar's head at Thomas Attree's dinner party – ILN 2 January 1847.

the kitchen. During Christmas 1846 Thomas Attree, a wealthy Brighton solicitor and public figure, entertained guests at his Queen's Park mansion at which the ceremony of parading the roasted boar's head was resurrected along with, said the *ILN*, a troupe of 'rustics' dressed in Alpine costumes acting out a masque. It was deemed worthy of a picture in the *ILN*. The verses celebrated the boar and the alleged Germanic origins of the tradition:

Greet our stranger, greet him well,
He comes your Christmas joys to swell;
Now Merry England care beguiles,
And wisdom nods and beauty smiles ;
And east and west, and south and north,
Pour their lavish treasures forth
From where the Rhine's blue rushing fleet
Whirls past the mighty Taurus' feet
Monarch of mountain, grove and pool
He comes to grace your feast of yule.

According to a contemporary recipe, if any guest around Attree's fastidiously arranged dining table actually sampled bits of the boar's head it should have been, first, singed to remove all the bristles, and then the bones, snout, brain and tongue removed, after which the residue should have been heavily seasoned, well boiled, and left to be served cold.

Christmas Present & Christmas Past

Interestingly, in its first Christmas edition published on Christmas Eve 1842 the *ILN* enthused over the appropriateness of the celebrations but failed to mention the birth of Jesus. It was relieved that the mild winter that year had eased the wretched lives of the poor, but railed against the new workhouse system – *the bastilles of England, the prisons rather than the shelter of the destitute of the land.* It said charity remained an essential element in national life, and hoped the clergy would encourage the rich *to seek by those personal virtues to atone for the wickedness of national severity and injustice....so that the light of their own festive happiness may carry a smiling reflection back into the cottage, and bless, without spilling one drop of the poison of envy into their bosoms, the grateful spirits of the poor.*

For most people, however, the *ILN* claimed that Christmas had come *hand in hand with Plenty and with Peace.* It was gratified that farming was prospering, food was getting cheaper, and the recent British wars against the Afghans (to secure a friendly Emir against Russian infiltration) and the Chinese (to compel them to open up trade, especially in opium) had been successful. It then descended to the realm of mockery saying it wished the emissary of the defeated Chinese emperor could experience an English Christmas. *How soon he would entwine his crown and plat his tails with holly and the red berry of the west.! How he would pour elder, and spiced ale, and flip* (cognac) *and ginger to be "hot i'the mouth", down his ambassadorial throat! How he would make plum-pudding the joss* (idol) *of his momentary veneration, and convince him of the improvement that is rendered unto mustard by beef!*

Elsewhere in its first Christmas edition the *ILN* tracked references across the centuries to Christmas celebrations at the English royal court. It noted the household records of expensive costumes, lavish food, copious drink and groups of musicians for the annual festivities from King Henry II (1154-89) onwards. They continued to be held by Henry VI (1422-61 and 1471-72), Edward IV (1461-71 and 1472-83) and Richard III (1483-85) during the episodic violence of the Wars of the Roses as they were tantamount to public statements of monarchical authority, stability and confidence. And as the royal palaces, and the castles of the aristocracy, were in essence busy towns they contained numerous retainers from

every social class from knights and squires to clerks, cooks, armourers and grooms. No doubt everyone benefited to a varying degree from the surging Christmas supply of food and drink, and accompanying revelry.

The *ILN* noted Henry VIII's (1509-47) love of extravagant masques and pageantry, and cited the contemporary historian John Stowe's (c1524-1605) description of a Tudor Christmas under the young Edward VI (1547-53). *There was in the feast of Christmas, in the King's house, wheresoever he was lodged, a Lord of Misrule or Master of Merry Disports, and the like had ye for the house of every nobleman of honour or good worship, were he spiritual or temporal, among the which the Mayor of London and either of their sheriffs had their several Lords of Misrule; you contending without quarrel or offence which should make the rarest pastimes to delight the beholders.* A Lord of Misrule was associated with the Roman Saturnalia, being the person elected to oversee and encourage events, and although there is no continuity between the legendary excesses of the Saturnalia and Tudor festivities the name was the same and so was the role.

Edward Corbould: Mummers performing before a medieval court – ILN 22 December 1866.

A Victorian montage of a medieval court at Christmas – ILN 25 December 1847.

In December 1866 the *ILN* featured *Mummers at Christmas in the Olden Times* by Edward Henry Corbould (1815-1905). It highlights the fantastical costumes and antics of the group, including the traditional young boy who announced the group to the household they were visiting and was responsible for collecting alms. They performed plays possibly, as here, incorporating tumbling and dancing, and presumably contributed much to the Christmas atmosphere of revelry. Although no records of specific plays by medieval mummers survive, those from the eighteenth century onwards often have some wild and eccentric figure representing Old Christmas in their stories, along with St George and assorted

woodland characters of charming, cruel and comic dispositions. Many groups faded away in the nineteenth century, mainly victims of puritanical criticisms of the morality of the characters and plot, but a few plays survived in localities to become the revered traditions of modern times.

The Idealised Middle Ages

When Queen Elizabeth I (1558-1603) was succeeded by James I (1603-25) and then Charles I (1625-49) the Lords of Misrule faded from view although they were never quite extinguished, but the Christmas masques, pageants and banquets orchestrated by possibly slightly more refined masters of the revels continued unabated at court and in great houses. No doubt behaviour varied widely, but as the *ILN* stated, *In the reign of Elizabeth the Puritans began to lift up their testimony against the pageantries of Christmas,* and as the Parliamentary forces gained the upper hand in the Civil War in the later 1640s so plays, the decoration of churches with evergreens, and finally the festival of Christmas itself were suppressed.

When Charles II was restored (1660-85), so was Christmas in all its variety, but said the *ILN* in December 1842, *in none of its ancient haunts did the festival ever again recover its splendour of old. In a word, the old English feeling seemed extinct, and the ancient customs which had connected themselves therewith one by one fell into more disuse. The Christmas festival has languished from those days to this; but never has been, and never will be, extinct. The stately forms of its celebration in high places have long since passed away; but the spirit of the season yet survives, and amid the carking anxieties of the busy world around us, this period of commemoration is invariably a merry time.* The *ILN* noted the survival of carol singing, the burning of a Yule Log (notably in northern counties), the gathering of holly, ivy and mistletoe, the acting out of a play celebrating St George and the Dragon (notably in western counties), the habit of the squire distributing modest largesse to villagers, and the popularity of goose and turkey.

On Christmas Day 1847 the *ILN* featured a montage of medieval Christmas scenes made to look like a secularised version of a pre-Reformation church chancel. A large triptych featured the Annunciation, the shepherds visiting the stable,

Florence Claxton: Utopian Christmas – ILN 24 December 1859.

and Mary showing Jesus to one of the Magi. Below it were collections of armour and weapons of war and hunting. Below them were three scenes. In the centre an altar engraved with people hauling a huge Yule log was replete with fruits of the earth and flagons of wine, with a pile of dead game in front. To the right the poor and infirm were queuing for the alms distributed by their lord, and to the left were the court's musicians, jester, and masked players for St George and the Dragon. Overall the picture symbolised the mix of religious observation, charitable deeds, and personal indulgence the Victorians thought characterised Christmas. And they took comfort from believing this was exactly how their forbears thought and behaved in the idealised medieval world so beloved by Victorian artists, architects and Anglican clergy promoting the Gothic Revival.

Utopian Christmas

On Christmas Eve 1859 *Utopian Christmas* by Florence Claxton (1838-1920) transferred the medieval baron's feasting and alms-giving in his castle to an awkward looking idealised banquet in a Victorian mansion – thereby at once highlighting the separateness of the classes in the mid-nineteenth century in contrast to the idealised social mixing and inter-dependency believed to govern medieval feudal society.

Scattered across the illustration aristocratic ladies and gentlemen in evening dress are ensuring the poor are welcomed, seated and fed while the orchestra plays and the royal family looks on. Everything about the illustration is formal and strained. It would have been well known that many of the wealthy mansion blocks and terraces of London and other cities were well guarded gated communities to keep the ordinary working classes, other than servants and visiting tradesmen, at a clearly marked distance. And the front door 'family' would rarely see the back door tradesmen or acknowledge servants.

George Dodgson: Christmas Eve in Yorkshire – ILN *1849 Christmas Supplement.*

A Servants' Hall on Christmas Eve

In its 1849 Christmas Supplement the *ILN* found some other traditions had survived. A picture by George Haydock Dodgson (1811-80) *drawn on the spot showed Merry-Making on Christmas-Eve in one of our northern counties. The scene is one of those large kitchens which are only to be found in some old English manor house. Supper is over, and all cleared away for the dance; drinking will go on until the Waits* (strolling carol singers) *come, which will be long after midnight,* *when the large table will once more be spread with refreshments, and the cup will continue to circulate until morning. Elder wine, spiced ale, and "egg-hot"* (hot ale frothed with eggs, brandy and sugar) *are the principle beverages drunk in the north of England on Christmas-Eve.* Joints and candles and mistletoe hang from the beams, the fire roars away, the local fiddler calls out the dances, and, while the drinking goes on, a chair crashes over as a man chases a girl up onto a dresser and another girl is kissed under the mistletoe.

Wassailing & Twelfth Night

In December 1881 the *ILN* noted the soaring interest in the surviving local Christmas traditions, and with sadness noted the decay of communal festivities from an allegedly better age as put into verse by Sir Walter Scott (1771-1832) in *Marmion*, his poem of sixteenth century love, jealousy and deceit published in 1808.

England was merry England, when
Old Christmas brought his sports again.
'Twas Christmas broached the mightiest ale;
'Twas Christmas told the merriest tale;
A Christmas gambol oft could cheer
The poor man's heart through half the year.

Among the remnants of communal festivities it noted that on the Isle of Man Christmas Eve carols were sung amidst flocks of sheep, in some Yorkshire villages children paraded through the streets with trumpets, drums and bells, across northern counties Yule logs were still cut and burned with due ceremony, in Worcestershire mummers still dressed in fantastic costumes and danced through the streets, and in several places people gathered around hives hoping to hear the bees humming at midnight to mark the birth of Jesus. The *ILN* noted that wassailing apple trees on Twelfth Night *was not quite obsolete* in western cider making counties. In the evening the farmers' family and friends gathered around the best tree in the orchard and placed cakes on the branches and poured cider over the roots in the hope of an excellent harvest. Among the variety of accompanying incantations was:

Stand fast root, bear well top,
Pray the God send us a good howling crop;
Every twig, apples big,
Every bough, apples enow –
Hats full, caps full,
Full quarters, sacks full.

The wassailing often occurred (and still does) on Old Twelfth Night – 17 January. In 1582 Pope Gregory XIII established the Gregorian calendar which rectified the errors in the Roman Julian one of 45BC. By 1582 the yearly error of 11 minutes and 14 seconds had accumulated to 10 days. While nearly all Roman Catholic countries immediately adopted the Gregorian calendar,

Protestant and Eastern Orthodox ones delayed doing so – Great Britain until 1752 when 2 September was followed by 14 September as by then the difference was 11 days. Many people, though, clung to the old calendar when it came to Christmas celebrations, with the Old Christmas Day of 6 January being preferred to the New Christmas Day of 25 December. (By the year 2000 the Old Christmas Day had moved 12 days away, to 7 January.) And as Pope Gregory had decreed that 1 January was New Year's Day (rather than as hitherto a date in March) from 1752 Great Britain's Old and New Christmas Days fell in different years.

On Christmas Eve 1842 the *ILN* pictured a white bearded old man draped in a billowing cloak with a holly wreath on his head rising out of a huge steaming bowl labelled 'Wassail'. Traditionally it was full of mulled cider and dried fruit. He was holding an evergreen branch and from his copious sleeve were falling a bottle of ale, a plum pudding and a pineapple. The title was *Old Christmas*, which referred not to the date but to the man himself. He *was* Old Christmas, dressed in green not red, and as the first verse of the accompanying poem made clear, he was of Classical not Christian ancestry:

They say that bright Venus, when she came to wean us
From prudence, and bind us to love, boy;
Blush'd up in a glow, from the sea-deeps below,
And took flight for the palace of Jove, boy!
Old Christmas was born on a frostier morn,
But with full as much warmth in his soul, sir;
Jove's nectar his sea; like a spirit-king he
Burst fresh into life from the bowl, sir!
From the bowl, sir!
Burst fresh into life from the bowl. sir!
Ho, ho! for Christmas! on island, sea or isthmus,
There's no old boy brings do much joy
As jolly, holly, Christmas!

The following year the Christmas edition featured Alfred Crowquill's sly looking Old Christmas with a long fluted glass and a grinning goblin in his hood. The accompanying commentary took the form of an imaginary Wassail Bowl procession into the communal feast with songs by minstrels and the master of ceremonies linking the food, drink and revelry to Old Christmas. The master of ceremonies sings

A revel! a revel! a rout! a rout!
"A Wassail" before the year is out
Honour the bowl! well wreathed around
With the green life, that doth abound
In dismal forests, when the trees
Shiver before the northern breeze

And the minstrels sing:

Old years have been – New years have been – and fleeted far away
Since first brave "Father Christmas" came, and caroll'd at the door;
He always found a cheerful cup, and a jesting word to say,
And a thousand fervent wishes – he deserves a thousand more.

Wassail Bowl and Old Christmas – ILN 24 December 1842.

Old Christmas and goblin – ILN 23 December 1843.

The Origins of the Wassail Bowl

In 1865 a lengthy article on the origin of the Wassail Bowl was accompanied by James Godwin's typically Victorian rendering of a key event in the distant story. It is about the year 450AD. The Romans had long gone, and Vortigen, the Christian British King had made a treaty with the pagan Saxons, Hengist and Horsa, to help him defeat the northern Picts in return for the grant of land in Lincolnshire. By agreement further Saxons arrived from overseas, and among them was Hengist's beautiful daughter Rowena. Vortigen visited Hengist in his new palace at Thancaitre where Rowena presented the king with a golden cup of wine saying 'Lauerd King, waes heil'. He replied courteously 'Drink Heil', and both drank from the cup, and thus was born the enduring Wassail custom of the greeting and drinking of each other's health. However the pagan Rowena beguiled the Christian Vortigern, and Hengist and Horsa encouraged their union in return for the Saxons being given possession of the Kingdom of Kent. Some years later Hengist and Horsa treacherously murdered many Saxon nobles at a feast, and Vortigern was captured and forced to cede Essex, Sussex and Middlesex. The *ILN* took the story largely from the dramatic if not trustworthy annals of the ninth century monk Nennius and and twelfth century cleric Geoffrey of Monmouth. It ends with fire falling from heaven and killing the weak-willed and sinful Vortigern along with Rowena and all the courtiers in their castle on the River Towey.

James Godwin: The Origins of the Wassail Bowl – ILN 23 December 1865.

Alfred Crowquill: Christmas – ILN *28 December 1844.*

Old Christmas Leads the Festive Procession

On 28 December 1844 a fantasy picture by Alfred Crowquill depicted his view of all things temporal contributing to Christmas revelry. It revealed the clear delineation between the religious observance of the Nativity and the communal festivities encouraged at mid-winter by Old Christmas. Happy children follow the flaming torch of the evergreen laden figure as he leads the turkey and goose and the anthropomorphised wassail bowl, plum pudding, mutton chop and rabbit to the festivities. Behind them come a dragon, clown and Punch from contemporary pantomimes, and looking on are a couple holding a banner noting the craze for the recently introduced Polka. The accompanying poem by another hand spoke of memories of a more inclusive age.

Oh! what delight it is to think of childhood's generous days!
The banquet of our parents dear, the "youl log's" flickering blaze;
Our brothers and our sisters – the laugh, the dance, the song,
And brave old servants, clustering near all in a faithful throng,

With little lively children, the darlings of the scene,
Like fairies frisking to the sound of harp and tambourine;
The wassail bowl, parading round, also the silver cup
That ended with the kitchen folks that all might have their sup!

So popular were such images as these, especially the humanised Christmas pudding and pantomime animals, that in later decades they appeared on numerous Christmas cards.

Alfred Crowquill was the pseudonym of Alfred Henry Forrester (1804-72) who was an experienced designer of theatrical backdrops and inventive cartoonist and book illustrator. He was particularly adept at creating disturbing fantasies, often for the *ILN*, and his visualisation of the world included extreme caricatures, alarming juxtapositions and bizarre changes of scale within the same illustration. A 'crowquill' was a steel pen with a fine nib which he used for his sketches, but a possible reason for his choice of name was a 'quill' used to 'crow' in the sense of satirising the absurdities he saw around him. More works by Crowquill appear in the chapters on pantomimes (page 144) and the world of fairies (page 153).

A New Song for Christmas

In December 1844 the *ILN* featured Frederick James Smyth's *Jolly Old Christmas*. With his beard dripping with wine, his hair adorned with bottles and glasses, and a large plum pudding in his hand, he epitomised early Victorian expectations of this bucolic figure – an incitement to alcohol fuelled revelry. An elf helps lift the glass to his lips, and a young couple dance on his free hand.

Songs ancient and modern were popular among the Victorians – at Christmas as at any other time. Family entertainments often centred around music making, not least because printing techniques were making sheet music readily available. The *ILN* published the words and music of many seasonal songs

In December 1844 the popular Irish composer Joseph Augustine Wade (1796-1845) wrote and set to music a song to accompany Frederick Smith's illustration. It greets Old Christmas as an eagerly awaited friend.

JOLLY OLD CHRISTMAS.

WRITTEN AND COMPOSED BY J. AUGUSTINE WADE.

II.

A welcome, old Christmas, a welcome once more—
  Though thy head be all frosty and chill,
Thy heart is as warm with its good kindly store
  Of Affections and Fondnesses still
As ev'n in the days of our earlier years,
When our smiles were more often—less frequent our tears,
We greeted thy coming, and happy were we
Thy evergreen Holly and Ivy to see !

CHORUS.

Then evergreen Holly and Ivy let's sing,
  The leaves that crown'd Bacchus old Jollity's King !

III.

What, tho' the sweet summer months have all sped,
  And silence is in their lone bow'rs—
What, tho' the roses are wither'd or fled,
  Still the Holly and Ivy are ours !

Oh ! thus in the winter of life may we feel,
An enjoyment that even cold Time cannot steal—
A still blooming thought of some joy that is gone,
That will light us and warm us by Memory's sun !

CHORUS.

The evergreen Holly and Ivy let's sing,
  The leaves that crown'd Bacchus, old Jollity's King !

J. Augustine Wade's Jolly Old Christmas – ILN 21 December 1844.

Kenny Meadows: Merry Christmas – ILN 25 December 1847.

An Incitement to Revelry

On Christmas Day 1847 a disconcerting illustration by Kenny Meadows featured a roaring Old Christmas pouring himself a libration. Ghostly figures floated within his flowing beard. Around him people were playing cards, drinking and eating in uninhibited fashion, laughing at a game of blind man's bluff, and a man was grabbing a woman around her head. The caption around Old Christmas – *Heaven Bless You, Merry Gentlefolk. Let Nothing You Dismay* – appears incongruous as giving God's approval of the cartoon's lascivious goings-on, but perhaps it was part of the convenient Victorian capacity to separate, or maybe interweave, the Christian and non-Christian aspects of this mid-winter festival. Or, far less likely, the *ILN* was pandering through titillating comedy to the moral rectitude of most of its readers.

A Favourite Figure in Transition

Victorian illustrators and writers found the mid-century transition perplexing as Christmas became more family centred, with children, domestic games, presents and fir trees taking centre-stage. The terminology was confusing too. In past centuries Old Christmas had been called Father Christmas or Lord Christmas, notably in pageants, masques and mummers' plays, and it was also another name for the Lord of Misrule. Whatever the name, this age-old 'person' had nothing to do with being kind to children, flying through the sky, going down chimneys or leaving presents. He was central to the romantic early nineteenth century concept of medieval England as a land where everyone was content with their place in society, where church and society worked in harmony for the common good, and where the rich looked after the poor. This revivalism brought

Charles Green: Old Father Christmas or The Cave of Mystery – ILN 22 December 1866.

Old Christmas back into prominence as the herald of Christmas revelry and symbolic bringer of good cheer. Numerous Victorian mummers incorporated him into their plays as the rumbustious leader of a festive group visiting families, telling stories, encouraging dancing, playing tricks on each other, and seeking alms.

In the second half of the nineteenth century his appearance gradually changed from the bucolic and sometimes grotesque and alarming presence to someone comfortingly like a favourite grandfather much concerned with children's happiness. Immigrants in the United State of America from northern Europe had brought with them Santa Claus from the Netherlands, Pelz Nickel from Germany, and Saint Nicholas from Russia. All were fur cloaked figures secretively bringing presents in the night for good children. The image was fed by numerous American books, but notably the famous poem *'Twas the Night before Christmas* first published in 1823, in which sleeping children are woken up by Saint Nicholas landing on the roof and coming down the chimney:

He was dressed all in fur, from his head to his foot,
And his clothes were all tarnished with ashes and soot.
A bundle of toys he had flung on his back,
And he looked like a pedlar, just opening his pack.
His eyes – how they twinkled! his dimples how merry!
His cheeks were like roses, his nose like a cherry!
His droll little mouth was drawn up like a bow
And the beard on his chin was as white as the snow.

He was chubby and plump, a right jolly old elf,
And I laughed when I saw him, in spite of myself!
A wink of his eye and a twist of his head,
Soon gave me to know I had nothing to dread.

By the 1850's the kindly figure was reaching the British Isles, and gradually the British Father Christmas lost his holly wreath and bottles, his cloak changed from green to fur edged red, his leery bucolic face became smiling and kind, and the Yule log he carried became a sack bursting with gifts. Rather confusingly, for a couple of decades both figures adorned magazines and newspapers, and sometimes it was difficult for observers to work out exactly whom they were looking at.

A clear example of this was *Old Father Christmas, or, The Cave of Mystery* by Charles Green (1840-98) featured on 22 December 1866. In it children gaze with a mixture of excitement and nervousness at the figure at the entrance to an enticing alcove. The commentary said the host had rejected the usual Christmas tree because when *the tapers wax dim – some of them, perhaps, going out splutteringly – the branches, despoiled of their goodly fruit, look gaunt, and grim, and scorched.* The cave, however, *appealed to the most most vivid part of youth's nature, at any rate, if not of human nature as a whole – the yearning after the vague and mysterious…The children trembling await the decision of the improvised Father Christmas, with his flowing grey beard, long robe, and slender staff – apt representative, in heart at any rate, of the veritable Christmas – whom they half believe and half doubt to be their host.* His purpose was akin to that of the imported and newly adopted Father Christmas but his appearance, with his holly wreath, straggly grey beard, goblin, staff, and leaner figure, looked more like Old Christmas.

Has Father Christmas arrived?

On New Year's Day 1881 a kindly looking bearded figure in a cloak was pictured holding a small girl clutching a a mix of fruit and grain in her apron. The artist was Alfred Edward Emslie (1848-1918). Old Christmas's evergreen wreaths have gone and so has the Wassail Bowl and invitation to drink. Emslie's figure seems like the new figure of Santa Claus imported from the United States of America, but perhaps he was a benign, sanitised and more generally acceptable 'modern looking' Old Christmas hoping the young New Year will turn out to be fertile and prosperous. The move to blend the two mystical figures – Santa Claus and Old Christmas – into the modern British Father Christmas was well under way.

Alfred Edward Emslie: The New Year – ILN *1 January 1881.*

CHAPTER THREE

That Special Christmas Dinner: The Best You Can Afford

Shopping developed apace in Queen Victoria's reign. Shops multiplied in number and in size as overseas trade and imports flourished, increasingly powerful steam locomotives hurried goods across the country, sophisticated technology ensured the range and quantity of products soared, and the rising middle classes had more money to spend and social aspirations to meet. The growing towns sucked in goods from an ever-widening circle of farms and factories, and the proliferation of urban horse drawn omnibuses allowed those without private carriages to seek out shops more easily. As the decades passed, people had a vast array of places offering them goods – from glittering department stores to market stalls. There were regular markets, ranging from the vast largely wholesale metropolitan fish, meat and poultry markets to the traditional general ones in town squares. There were an array of town shops with their own specialisms, such as grocers, bakers, butchers and haberdashers, and most of them undertook home deliveries by horse and cart. Homes – at least the middle class ones – were getting more comfortable. Ironmongers stocked an ever increasing range of manufactured goods, and numerous catalogues offered the sale and delivery of furniture, carpets and other heavy goods from manufacturers and retailers. There were, too, numerous businesses dealing in second-hand goods of every description, and indeed right down to third-hand and fourth-hand. Little was wasted, nearly everything had a value and could be recycled and resold, and food products had no sell-by dates.

Consumerism soared, and notably so in the second half of the century. Advertising flourished, and as it was unregulated great claims could be made for products, especially medicine and cosmetics. Everything in the Victorian world – a fashionable interest in life in an idealised past, a heightened

sense of family, vastly improved transport on land and sea, an expanding middle class with money and time to spare, and the creation of mass production techniques – contributed to Christmas becoming a retailer's delight.

Old Newgate Market on Christmas Eve

Illustrations on 27 December 1845 by William Linton (1812-97) featured the ancient Newgate and Leadenhall meat markets. Although well-patronised by retailers, hoteliers and the general public, Newgate market was basically a lengthy, malodorous, and unhygienic open-sided shed with hooks suspended from beams. Some animals were killed outside London and their carcasses hurried in by train or cart, but many were brought

William Linton: Newgate Market on Christmas Eve – ILN 27 December 1845.

in live on trains, wagons or coaches, or on their own feet, and slaughtered in cellars or sheds on site. Many women as well as men were employed as slaughterers and carriers. Newgate's reputation as a market remained high but by 1845 Newgate Street was increasingly criticised as an offensive nuisance. In Linton's picture sprigs of greenery attempt to give a festive feel, and maybe a more pleasant smell, as families and animals wander about the stalls. In 1868 most of Newgate's businesses transferred to the new purpose-built market facilities at Smithfield.

The *ILN*'s poem on Newgate Market includes the following verses – one of which avers to the bitter controversy caused by the recent abolition of the tax on imported corn by Sir Robert Peel, the Prime Minister.

Ribs, ribs by thousands, every kind
 Of British beef is there
A lady buys a monstrous round
 To send to Russell square

Mutton – Ah, yes, in every form
 Upon the light it drops
The horseman eyes his saddle
 The beggar smacks his chops

Vela, veal, Oh veal, we leave to Peel
 The Common weal or woe;
But isn't it sweet to see the meat
 Adorned with mistletoe!

And doesn't it look, hung high on hook,
 Quite greaseful near the holly,
And when we pay, doesn't the tray
 That bears it home look jolly.

By day or night this mart is light,
 Oh let no mortal dark it;
For in Christmas time it seems sublime,
 To buy at Newgate Market.

Leadenhall Market at Christmas

Leadenhall Market near Fenchurch Street was another centuries-old trading centre for a wide variety of provisions – meat, game, poultry, fish, eggs and grain. Largely rebuilt after the Great Fire of 1666, the market had three covered halls fitted out with traders' beams, benches and cellars. The Beef Market specialised in leather, raw hides, baize and wool as well as beef. The Greenyard had room for 140 stalls selling veal, mutton, lamb and poultry. The third hall was the Herb Market. Nearby passages housed numerous shops trading in other provisions, notably cheese and fish.

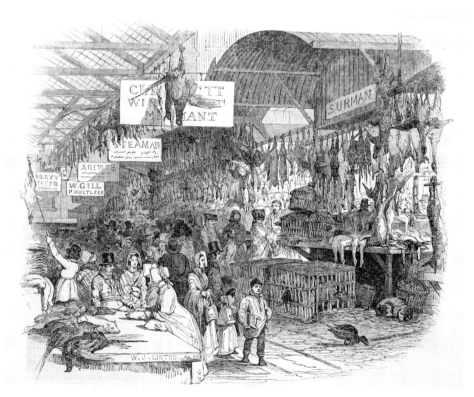

William Linton: Leadenhall Market at Christmas – ILN 27 December 1845.

The *ILN* featured visitors to the massive poultry section as Christmas approached, and gives some impression of the massive stocks, and the mixed clientele circulating in the less than hygienic conditions. Most animals and poultry had been slaughtered, but some were still alive in the wicker baskets. This sprawling market was increasingly seen as an unacceptably offensive sight in the city, and was rebuilt in ornate style in 1881. However many traders found its rents prohibitive and preferred to use the new Smithfield premises. The *ILN*'s poem celebrated the Christmas hurly-burly.

The market wide of Leadenhall
 I seek as I'm a sinner
Where people make a Christmas din
 In buying Christmas dinner

Why all the City I declare
 Has thither swept its tide
Behold its poultry and its crowd
 That walk on the Cheap-side

Come buy! buy! buy! the tradesfolk cry
 With emphasis quite clever
Oh bi! bye! bie! by! boi! bli! buy!
 Ma'am now your time or never!

In all probability the reformed Scrooge sent to Leadenhall Market for the plump turkey to give to the Cratchit family on Christmas Day.

The Norfolk Game Coach

The 1845 Christmas issue pictured a stagecoach arriving from Norfolk, but filled with dead game for sale rather than passengers. As the accompanying poem said, the days of stagecoaches as carriers of passengers were numbered as more and more sections of the Norwich to London railway line were completed. Its full opening as a through line was celebrated on 15 December that year.

Ah! coaches once were all the go,
 With passengers a-top;
Now, that would not be safe – because
 The nation's let them drop!

The coach was becoming little more than a carrier's cart. With simple plays on words, the poem celebrates the residual importance of the coach at Christmas.

It is a Christmas coach, I vow,
 And whirls along in pride;
For all its outside passengers
 Are food for the inside

Turkey and pullet ride and tie
 Game, poultry, cheek by jowl;
I wonder who was game to pay
 The fare for so much fowl!

But only think when they're at home,
 Admired, pluck'd, and spitted,
On tables free, how they will be
 To highest ranks admitted.

In December 1846 the *ILN* noted 2,400 geese had been driven along the roads of Norfolk from Boston, and fed from sacks of corn all the way, to be slaughtered by a Spalding dealer for sale in London. By then the vast quantities of birds and animals earmarked for Christmas dinners in London, and other large Victorian cities, had arrived in a number of ways. Many arrived alive by trains as the railway network spread, but the historic custom of driving flocks

The Norfolk Game Coach – ILN 27 December 1845.

or herds on foot all the way to market remained common. Not surprisingly, on arrival the latter needed fattening up for a few weeks to fetch the best price. Farmers had to decide upon the cheapest option.

Catching the Coach

Fifteen years later, on 21 December 1861, an illustration by Edward Duncan (1803-82), a noted landscape and marine artist, showed two country lads waiting to add their catch of rabbits and pheasants to an approaching coach. Someone on it will do business with them. By that date railways dominated long distance travel and most of the horse drawn coaches still in business were reduced to local connecting services or being little more than carriers' carts.

ILN readers may well have wondered whether the lads were the legal owners of the game or had been poaching in some great landowner's woods. Poaching by local families with inadequate earnings was common, and also by professional gangs working on a far larger scale. By the 1860s the days of man traps set to crush a poacher's leg had gone, but armed gamekeepers on great estates still kept watch by day and night and injuries still occurred when they encountered gangs prepared to fight when cornered. Rabbits were common victims of poachers traps, but pheasants specially bred on estates for shooting parties were the greater prize – both in terms of the poacher's pride and financial returns. Few poor rural families saw poaching as a crime – it could be a necessity, but was often seen as a sporting challenge and as a satisfying snub to the ruling classes.

Edward Duncan: Waiting for the Coach – ILN *1861 Christmas Supplement.*

The Late Arrival

The railways did not always guarantee a prompt delivery During the bitter Scottish railway strike in the winter of 1890-91 an illustration showed a table laid with the butler showing his irate master a turkey delayed in transit and rendered inedible.

The picture highlighted the accusation levied by many in Scotland that the railwaymen deliberately attempted to wreck Christmas. As the conflict between the employees and directors of the Caledonian Railway Company reached crisis point in late December 1890 there may well have been truth in the accusation. When the directors refused to consider going to arbitration over the demands for a ten hour day and other reforms the railwaymen went on strike without warning on 22 December.

Across much of Scotland coal and other supplies came to a sudden halt, and widespread violence broke out when the directors sought to bring in non-union labour and eject strikers from their homes. Christmas made little difference to the bitterness or the strikers attacks on stations, signal boxes and sidings. The *ILN*, in common with many across Scotland at the festive season, displayed no sympathy with the strikers, noting *The retail price of coal was doubled, and great distress was brought upon the poorer classes.*

Only at the end of January 1891 did emotions cool when the Scottish grandee, the Earl of Aberdeen, the much respected Lord Lieutenant of Aberdeen, mediated an agreement which effectively granted the railwaymen their demands – and showed all other trades unions what could be achieved through unity and determination. The 'Christmas railway strike' was a seminal moment in the nation's deteriorating industrial relations.

J. Walter Wilson: Late Arrival of the Christmas Turkey on New Year's Day – ILN *10 January 1891.*

An Economical Christmas

On 21 December 1878 an illustration by Walter Jenks Morgan (1847-1924) pinpointed the thrift with which various sections of society were obliged to approach Christmas, and especially the purchase of meat. It is Saturday night in the new London Poultry Market, and the dealer is selling off *the surplus supply of plump geese and turkeys, chickens and ducklings, wild fowl, hares and rabbits, partidges, plovers and other delicacies. Here are thrifty housewives, mothers of families, landladies of suburban lodgings, bachelors of epicurean taste but of economical* principles, who dine at home on the day of rest, and are disposed to save a shilling, careful working men who fancy they can teach their wives a lesson in household management, and small retailers whose business in their own neighbourhood will begin at a later hour, to go on briskly until the stroke of midnight. The *ILN* said, *It may be unfashionable, or even "low", but it is cheap and safe and not unwise.* The top hats, well-fitting and far from threadbare jackets, and well-dressed mother and child point to a largely thrifty and respectable section of society who found the experience profitable and satisfying rather than something of which to be ashamed.

Walter Jenks Morgan: Saturday Night in the Metropolitan Poultry Market
– ILN *21 December 1878.*

What's Left

There were many people experiencing far greater hardship than those flocking to the Poultry Market evening sale.

In 1889 the *ILN* chose its 28 December edition to print a thought provoking picture by Everard Hopkins (1860-1928). It showed the poor – one girl and boy barefooted – gathered in the cold of the night with empty baskets and anxious faces outside a fishmonger's and poulterer's shop in the hope they could afford some left-overs. A well dressed mother and child looking straight ahead pass them by, as does the hansom cab. No commentary was included or needed. The title said it all – *"What's Left" or Crumbs from the Rich Man's Table.*

Everard Hopkins: "What's Left" or Crumbs from the Rich Man's Table – ILN 28 December 1889.

Alfred Hunt: The Compliments of the Season – ILN 16 December 1871

The Compliments of the Season

As Christmas 1871 approached, the *ILN* published *The Compliments of the Season* by the prolific landscape artist Alfred Hunt (1830-96). With heavy humour the commentary says the richly attired sisters and their brother are returning to their mansion from a charitable walk in the village and as they passed a farm on their estate they were *suddenly accosted by Signor Gallipavo. Of him it may be said, as Master Fabian says of Malvolio in the play of "Twelfth Night" – "Contemplation makes a rare turkey-cock of him: see how he jets under his advanced plumes."* William Shakespeare mentioned them in *Act II, Scene V* of this play which was first performed about 1602.

Wild turkeys were originally termed *Gallipavo Mexicania,* and the commentary asserts this fine turkey's Spanish American ancestry *has bequeathed him such a heritage of pride!* Much like a preening grandee such as Malvolio, *with head erect in conscious dignity, wearing the adornment of a rubicund comb on his lofty brow, his pendent wattles of a sanguine hue, and a very splendid scarlet gorget all down his noble neck, what a lordly visage he rears above the mighty orb of his ample breast! ... He considers himself a very good-looking bird, as he struts*

forward, modestly followed by his demure female consort. Arrogant and self-deluded, he exchanges haughty compliments of the season with the family, and graciously accepts their invitation to join them on Christmas Day. *He means to make himself quite agreeable to the company. In this, we are sure, there will be no disappointment.* A turkey looking forward to Christmas was as much a joke to the Victorians as it is now. And most Victorian families were used to animals being killed on farms, in back yards, at markets, and by local butchers.

Turkeys came from the Americas and were first brought to England by Tudor sailors in the 1520s. However wealthy Tudors and Stuarts enjoyed peacock and swan, sometimes preluded by a boar's head paraded through the hall, and the goose remained the commonest Christmas meal well into Victorian times, largely because it was the cheaper option (and, some thought, the tastier). The name 'turkey' may have attached itself to them because, erroneously, they were thought to be related to the common guinea fowl which were generally known as Turkey Coqs or Turkey Hennes. The birds were traded by Turkish Levantine merchants and this, too, may account for the name.

*Lucien Davis: No Admittance
– ILN 19 December 1885.*

No Admittance – Except on Business

On 19 December 1885 two pictures by Lucien Davis (1860-1941) no doubt amused Victorian readers. The first showed a girl and a dog fiercely denying a wandering goose entry to the house, and the second showed the same girl and dog looking longingly at the same goose – cooked.

ILN readers would have appreciated the pictures sly reference in the title *No Admittance – Except on Business* to the class conscious Victorian adage that tradesmen might be acceptable on business but were never suitable to receive socially.

Lucien David: Except on Business –
ILN *19 December 1885.*

Hablot Knight Browne (Phiz) The Goose Club – ILN 24 December 1853.

The Goose Club Draw

Although there were many imported geese, as well as home bred ones, their price was beyond most working class families and Goose Clubs, usually organised by local publicans, provided a way of spreading the cost over several months. Workers paid in weekly amounts, the publican raised the geese for a fee, or more likely purchased them from a wholesaler, and at Christmas a draw was held. A goose was held up, a ticket was drawn and its owner had that goose – whatever it was like. The opportunity for fraud was clear but the clubs proved popular

and no doubt shrewd members kept a close eye on the organiser. Most likely a significant proportion of the publican's profit came from the extra drink sold at the draw. On Christmas Eve 1853 the *ILN* featured a drawing by Hablot Knight Browne (1815-82) of a crowded Goose Club Draw and a couple of its fortunate and less-fortunate members.

Browne used the pen name Phiz after he met and befriended Charles Dickens in 1836 and began to illustrate his novels – including *The Pickwick Papers*, *David Copperfield*, *Dombey & Son*, *Martin Chuzzlewit* and *Bleak House*.

Foraging for a Christmas Dinner

On 21 December 1867 the savage illustration *Foraging for a Christmas Dinner* featured a fox in the process of killing a chicken in a farmyard outhouse. The artist was George Bouverie Goddard (1832-86) who specialised in field-sports, and no doubt agreed with the commentary which fully excused the fox, despite its habit of slaughtering far more poultry than it ate. *An animal which furnishes so much sport may well take some licence where landlords don't put up proper poultry houses for their tenants and tenants do not care to do it for themselves. Still, the amount of injury done is sadly exaggerated, and hunt funds have paid for many a lamb and rooster on which no fox ever laid tooth or pad.* Hunts, largely funded by wealthy owners of estates generally expected tenant farmers to be tolerant of damage done to hedges, fences and crops and not to hunt down and shoot foxes themselves – for which due recompense was often made by the hunt committee.

Boxing Day saw numerous hunt meetings, and in celebration of the 144 packs of fox hounds across the nation, the *ILN* asserted: *In fact, the fox is the very pivot on which country matters turn, as it is the secret spring of half the balls, dinners and breakfasts. It gives boundless employment to corn, straw and hay dealers; to builders, joiners, saddlers, tailors, blacksmiths, horsedealers, earth stoppers, hunt servants, and grooms immeasurable; spurmakers rejoice because of it; and yet its only honour after death is to stand stuffed in a saddler's window or a lobby, to peep out above a ball orchestra from a circlet of "evergreen gorse", and to dust furniture with its brush.* The fox's good reputation was fragile, though, and depended entirely on the excitement it offered. *If he flies across the country for his life he is termed "a gallant straight-necked fellow'. If he will not break cover, and prefers running the risk of a fox-hound's jaws at every turn, he is straightway called "a ringing, cowardly brute."*

George Bouverie Goddard: Foraging for a Christmas Dinner – ILN 21 December 1867.

Christmas Fruit

On 22 December 1849 a busy illustration showed Christmas fruit being unloaded at Cox's Wharf, not far downstream from London Bridge. The river, quay and upper counting house were to the left, with the vast warehouses across the middle cart-way. Fast schooners were now bringing in around 250 million oranges a year. This year's supply was *remarkably fine and abundant*, but great quantities of figs *were out of condition, from the length of the voyage*. Timing was everything. Valentia Raisins were in short supply with just 2,250 tons landed this season, but imported currants had reached an all-time record of almost 4,000 tons. The *ILN* noted that the welcome reduction in import duty had led to the consumption of currants doubling in seven years.

Twenty-five years later, on Boxing Day 1874 an illustration featured stevedores at London Bridge's Fresh Wharf, some wearing the traditional load-bearing padded hats, laboriously winching and carrying boxes of oranges from a finely detailed cargo vessel. By the 1870s many cargo vessels possessed auxiliary stream power to

Unloading fruit at Cox's Wharf, London Bridge – ILN 22 December 1849.

supplement their sails as the weather dictated and maintain their timetables. The commentary celebrated the vast overseas trade now associated with Christmas, with Fresh Wharf itself devoted to fruit from the Mediterranean, Azores and Canary Islands. *Let us only think of the plums and currants, the raisins and almonds, the figs, the oranges and lemons, the nuts of different kinds, the spices of various aromatic potency, the sugar for every description of sweetmeat and sweetening, the wines and liqueurs, and the miscellaneous groceries, which enter into the consumption of a bounteous household.*

Unloading oranges at Fresh Wharf, London Bridge – ILN 26 December 1874.

The Grocer's Shop at Christmas

In its Christmas Day issue in 1852 the *ILN* revealed how commerce was both fulfilling and exploiting the increasingly popular festive dinner. The illustration by Henry Anelay (1817-83) highlights the brightly lit grocer's shop as evening falls crowded with people from across the social classes. Flower, holly and mistletoe sellers are taking advantage of the Christmas crowd, the shop has employed a bill-board man to advertise its plum pudding ingredients, and ragged children are literally scraping the barrel of some comestible.

Many shops affect a peculiar style of decoration at Christmas time. The pastrycooks turn their counters into miniature plantations of fir-trees, that are laden with wax tapers and endless bonbon boxes ... The buttermongers throw up in their shop-windows wonderful masses of fortifications, with cannon peeping through port-holes, and sentinels leaning over parapets – the entire work constructed of the most massive cheese and butter; whilst beautiful white swans, made out of lard, swim about in a cool lake of real water in front of a rock of Stilton. The greengrocers

present an impenetrable thicket of holly and evergreens. The butchers delight in ornamenting their stock with bunches of ribbons and rosettes of the gayest colours, as if the animals had laid their heads with pride upon the butcher's block.

But we are almost inclined to believe that the grocers make the best Christmas display of all the London shopkeepers...We have seen many a shop-window that might vie in splendour with the last scene of a pantomime. It glittered all over with spangles, like a harlequin's dress. Some which we have admired in common with a whole Fop's-alley of fascinated boys, hang out a crystal curtain, in glorious emulation of Jullien's bal masque; and the effect is so dazzling that you can see to set your watch on the opposite side of the way. The celebrated impresario Louis Antoine Jullien (1812-60) conducted a series of winter masquerade balls at Covent Garden from 1844 onwards. They were hugely popular, and made more so by the sketches of Alfred Crowquill.

The *ILN* noted, though, that many of the grandest grocer's shops existed in poorer neighbourhoods. *There it is not unusual to count as many as twenty gas-lights burning the whole length of the shop, and*

Henry Anelay: The Grocer's Shop at Christmas – ILN 25 December 1852.

the effect of these is repeated in all directions by the contrivance of chandelier-drops and looking glasses, until the shops by the side of it look quite gloomy and black, like the cavern entrance before you plunge into the sea of light of Vauxhall Gardens. The comparison was apposite. Readers of the *ILN* would have known Lambeth's Vauxhall Gardens as a brightly lit pleasure park with refreshments, sideshows and entertainments, but also possessing lengthy unlit walks famous as places for discreet amorous encounters.

All the Trappings of Christmas

On 27 December 1873 the *ILN* gently mocked the lower middle class families making the best of their income, and in doing so it gave a glimpse into their likely lifestyle. They could enjoy, and display to family and friends, all the trappings of Christmas and then, maybe, quietly hide the price to be paid in terms of sparser fare the following week. *The bustle of laying in the required stock of kitchen, cellar, and cupboard stores for the convivial comforts of jolly old Christmas is the occasion of much pleasant excitement in a middle-class household where the mistress is not above going herself to market, and willing to let her children go with her. It may possibly, happen, too, that the husband and father can spare an hour of his working day to accompany the wife of his youth upon this agreeable errand, in which she is likely to find good cause for levying upon his ready purse a few shillings of extra taxation. For the purchase of a turkey and sausages, with herbs for stuffing, and a round of suet, raisins, and currants for the plum-pudding, with aromatic spices, and oranges and lemons, not to speak of a bottle of cognac brandy, has often come to more money than the amount of her previous estimate. ... And the arrears may perhaps be made up in future by nearly a week's dining (only herself and the children, for he takes his chop in town) on the remains of a Sunday boiled leg of mutton, to be served cold on the Monday and Tuesday, part hashed on the Wednesday, and part, with the bone, incorporated in a stew of meat and vegetables which will not be wholly consumed on the Thursday, but will reappear on the Friday's table.* However, with her husband home at the weekend, cutlets and a roast joint will appear followed by an apple-pie. *Such is life! and he would be an ungrateful fellow who would presume to murmur at this fare provided from an income of £300 or £400 a year, with several boys and girls to be fed as well as clothed and schooled, besides the house-rent and other costs of a modest domestic establishment.* Using the retail price index as a calculator, £350 in

Families at the Christmas market – ILN 27 December 1873.

1873 would represent a net income of around £32,000 today, but in those days food and clothing were more expensive in real terms, and rents less so than today. In 1873 nearly all schools charged fees, although they varied widely; today a free state school would be readily available.

Fetching Home the Christmas Dinner

In the 1848 Christmas Supplement *Fetching Home the Christmas Dinner* by John Leech (1817-64), the celebrated comic illustrator, pictured a scene that occurred every Sunday and not just at Christmas. People without kitchens paid a local baker to cook their rare hot meals in his ovens. Notwithstanding this sign of relative poverty, the commentary notes that some customers are particularly proud of their Christmas fare and have dressed as smartly as possible for the occasion. A goose, or more likely merely part of it, with mashed turnip and potatoes and a splash of apple sauce, followed

John Leech: Fetching Home the Christmas Dinner – ILN 1848 Christmas Supplement.

by a small home-made plum pudding and a bottle of beer was often the working class Christmas dinner.

From its socially superior standpoint the *ILN* remarked *It is not every day of the week or year that the poor can dine, and however vulgar may be the snob that arrays himself in his best on Christmas Day and brings home his dinner steaming hot from the convenient shop of Rusk, the baker, it would be both churlish and snobbish in us, or anyone else, to look with unsympathetic eyes, or turn up our noses contemptuously, upon the harmless and well-won enjoyment.* In fact the *ILN* praised their industry and thrift in saving up for Christmas and happily enjoying the day as they hurry home. Even here the gradations of society are clear. *Look at the venerable old lady – the occupant, doubtless, of an attic, or two-pair back, in some squalid street hard by. Doubtless in her humble household one awaits her coming with whom her modest feast is to be shared.* The *ILN* notes, too, the girl on the extreme left selling hot potatoes from the heated cylindrical potato-can, together with the thin young lad the *ILN* thinks she may have taken pity on.

Making the Christmas Pudding

The 1848 Christmas Supplement contained two pictures by Kenny Meadows of a mother and six excited children stirring the plum pudding and then placing it wrapped in a cloth in the boiler to steam. The family look wealthy enough to possess what appears to be a servant, and the *ILN* is pursuing the new found tradition that creating the pudding for Christmas is a whole household affair and, at its best, full of meaning. The plums – actually raisins – have to be selected and placed in the bowl, a task much prized by the children as a reward for good behaviour. And other ingredients reminded them of the world itself. *Raisins! They recall Turkey, and its men with long gowns, black beards, crooked scimitars, dark sparkling eyes, to say nothing of Giauors, Zuleikas, Bulbuls and gardens of roses. Currants! They suggest Greece, and the Levant, and the old Greek city, which gave their names to these berries. Spice! That is still better: the word conjures up all Arabia, Sinbad the Sailor, and fine old Harroun-al-Rashid. Sugar! The word is suggestive of Jamaica, hot suns, Jim Crow, and old Dan Tucker. Milk, Eggs, Fresh Butter! These remind [them] of the country, and of rambles in the fields for buttercups and daisies... Flour! This suggests the sturdy miller and the millstream, and the miller's daughter, 'Fairest of them all'. Lemon-peel! That recalls groves of citrons and oranges. Suet! That is the most disagreeable reminiscence: but even that, with a little effort, may be turned to pleasurable account; and the live oxen climbing the sunward hills may do duty for the butcher's shop.* The sweet smelling pudding was made round as, eulogised the *ILN*, *a kiss is round, the horizon is round, the earth is round, the moon is round, the sun and stars and all the host of heaven are round.*

Giauors were Christians, and evil-doers in Muslim eyes. Byron's 1813 poem 'The Giaour' used the term to describe the wild 'outsider' loved by the Turkish concubine Leila.
Zuleikas described beautiful Muslim women.
Bulbuls were colourful songbirds.
Corinth was the Greek city linked to currants.
Harroun-al-Rashid (the Just) ruled much of the Middle East from c786 to 809, and is included in the fictional One Thousand & One Nights.
At this time Jim Crow was a jovial African-American character played on the stage by the white actor Thomas Rice. From the 1880s the name became associated with America's punitive segregation laws.
'Old Dan Tucker' was a minstrel's song about a

Kenny Meadows: A Family Affair: Stirring the Christmas Pudding – ILN 1848 Christmas Supplement.

Kenny Meadows: Boiling the Christmas Pudding – ILN 1848 Christmas Supplement.

black man's wild behaviour in town.
There is nothing in this article to remind readers of the old recipes for plum pudding – especially those containing a great deal of meat, and those with the whole pudding stuffed into animal intestines much like the Scottish haggis. The sweet 1848 ingredients were key components of relatively new recipes, perhaps just a couple of decades old, but already becoming firmly attached to Christmas. Whether Prince Albert introduced the relatively meat-free variety is open to argument as possibly it was Queen Victoria's Hanoverian forebears in the eighteenth century, but undoubtedly the Victorians popularised it.

In due course the medieval festive 'luck tokens' reappeared as threepenny or sixpenny silver coins buried in the pudding. And Stir-up Sunday became another 'new tradition' adroitly linking faith, family and festivities. The collect (a prayer for a specific Sunday or Festival) for the Sunday before Advent contained the words *Stir up, we beseech thee, O Lord, the wills of thy faithful people; that they, plenteously bringing forth the fruit of good works, may of thee be plenteously rewarded.* As the Christmas pudding mixture needed several weeks to mature this fortuitous Sunday became the occasion for the family to get-together to 'stir-up' all the ingredients. A wooden spoon was used in remembrance of Christ's crib, and the stirring had to be clock-wise for luck.

Serving the Christmas Pudding

As early as 23 December 1843 the *ILN* featured the family's cook, beset by eager dogs and children, bringing in the Christmas pudding – round and topped with a sprig of holly. The picture, by Frederick James Smyth (fl 1841-67), belies the assumption that Victorian children were the paradigms of decorum, and might be seen but should never be heard.

And as the *ILN*'s illustration *The Pudding in Peril* reveals, the ceremony of bringing in the Christmas pudding, and setting light to a covering of cognac brandy, was a well-established 'tradition' by 1876. Although superficially humorous, the alarming

Frederick James Smyth: Christmas at Home' – ILN *23 December 1843.*

illustration was yet another *ILN* metaphor for the uncertainties of life and how a family's happiness could be shattered by instant calamity.

Dogs were important to the Victorians, and not only those bred as hunters and retrievers but also those beloved as domestic pets for their playfulness and companionship. In paintings they were usually symbols of unquestioning devotion and steadfastness, and many Victorian stories centred on the loyalty and heroism of dogs, even to the point of sacrificing their lives. Here they are treated rather differently. Smyth included them as excited family compatriots celebrating Christmas, while Gregory featured one as the pampered article of destruction – hopefully averted.

Victorian Christmas card with a box of bon–bon shaped Christmas crackers (author's collection).

Christmas Crackers

The Christmas cracker was the creation of Tom Smith (1823-69) an enterprising London confectioner. Introduced in the 1840s just as Christmas festivities were expanding across the middle classes, it started as a sweet, usually the popular sugared almond, wrapped in a twist of paper. It was copied from the French bon-bon. In due course a motto was added but it took a decade or more for the explosive 'cracker' element to be safely added inside the familiar lengthy cardboard tube. Legend claimed that Smith had the idea of the satisfying 'crack' after watching a crackling log fire.

Very soon boxes of crackers were advertised with a variety of 'gifts' inside them to suit every pocket and occasion, but try as he might Smith and his successors never achieved many sales outside Christmas. He had, though, created an almost instant Christmas tradition – based purely on commercial profit.

Charles Gregory: The Pudding in Peril – ILN Christmas Number 1876.

CHAPTER FOUR

Going to Church at Christmas:
Appearances and Aspirations

It seems safe, if maybe surprising, to conclude that much about Christmas in Victorian times was not to do with religion. It had a great deal to do, though, with the celebration of family life, and getting together with friends, sharing a special festive meal, enjoying parlour games and pantomimes, and sparing a thought for the very poor. As it evolved, it seized upon threads of age-old myths and legends in the form of the Old Christmas and Wassailing, the drinking and feasting linked to them, the symbolism of various evergreens use as decorations in ancient times, and assorted songs of the past, and turned them into adjuncts of a whole-hearted mid-winter celebration centred upon an important Christian festival, although that festival was far from being the most important one in the religious calendar. Good Friday, Easter and the Ascension always have been given primacy by the Roman Catholic and Protestant Churches.

The birth of Jesus lay at the heart of Christmas, as no doubt nearly everyone acknowledged, and many people went to church on Christmas Day, and perhaps more than went regularly each Sunday. Interestingly the 1851 national census included a unique section on church attendance, and although it had its faults – such as not recognising that some people attended more than once on the selected Sunday in May, and that some ministers may have merely guessed numbers – it showed that 10.89 million attendances were recorded from a population of 17.9 million people who were estimated as capable of attending (ie excluding the infirm or very young). It seems, at most, around 55% of the relevant population attended church – a high figure compared with today – but it is reasonable to assume that many more people, like today, were happy to enjoy Christmas (at some sort of level) without an act of worship.

Nevertheless, although the *ILN* primarily reflected the secular aspects of the festival, it did not entirely neglect churches and carols at Christmas, but sometimes the commentary was perhaps not quite what the reader expected.

Rural Virtues

Two illustrations appeared on the same page on 19 December 1868. *Christmas Morning* by Samuel Read (1815-83) pictured villagers walking through snowy fields to church, and *Christmas Night* inscribed C. Robinson (possibly John Charles Robinson 1824-1913) showed city dwellers walking home in the freezing cold after an evening's festivities. Beauty, calm and contentment shine through the former; ugliness, ice and threat besmirch the latter. Of the former the commentary eulogises the church: *See how it stands with its ivy-grown tower uplifting a modest spire, which ever points skyward, as who should say, "There! that's your way, good people! Up with you, and bless you!"* The spacious porch, too, welcoming and sheltering all the inhabitants of the village, the old and young, rich and poor, gentle and simple... The *ILN* was doing what so many Victorians commentators did, which is enthuse about an idealised rural society at the expense of a frighteningly chaotic urban one. *Indeed there is no incident in this home-like English rural scene which may not yield instruction to the thoughtful observer. The leafless elms and willows, patiently awaiting the genial return of spring; the ancestral yew-trees, unwithering, unchanging, a perpetual guardian of the graves of the dead; the quiet sheep in the field; the still pool at the roadside; the very smoke of the squire's plenteous kitchen, which pours out of the lofty chimney; the most trivial circumstances here portrayed are in keeping with the even tenor of that peaceful village life. Such is the life of these good folks who we now see reverently pacing to their church on Christmas morning.* The city at night is far less comforting, and the implication is that urban families, many of whom were first generation immigrants from rural communities, were without the moral compass allegedly associated with traditional country patterns of life. It was therefore easy to be led astray as maybe was happening to this young family. *It is the third hour past midnight. The snow, flying wildly in the frequent gusts of a north-west wind, that lashes the face and tears open the folds of clothing, has already laid a white carpet on the chill pavement, while these belated foot-passengers were eating their supper, or while Miss Anna, who now shivers despite her muff and shawl, was polking with Harry Johnson.* (The polka had reached England in the mid-1840s) *Papa keeps his own breast warm by carrying little Matty, fast asleep in his manly arms; while Mama is hooded and muffled in her thick plaid, but feels dreadfully anxious about coughs and face-aches on the morrow.*

C. Robinson: Christmas Night – ILN *19 December 1868.*

Samual Read: Christmas Morning – ILN *19 December 1868.*

Alfred Hunt: A Christmas Present to the Vicar – ILN *26 December 1874.*

A Christmas Present to the Vicar

On Boxing Day 1874 a strikingly busy illustration by Alfred Hunt (1830-96) featured the spacious well-fitted parlour of a comfortable country parsonage where the vicar and his family have just received the gift of a Christmas hamper of game from the local squire. This is not charity but a present based upon respect between families of high social standing in the locality, although the gift could be seen as subtly intimating the squire held the superior position. The clergyman is well-dressed and so are his numerous children ranging between the grown-up daughter reading the donor's letter and the child in the high chair with the attached toy horse. The females are excited by the hamper, but the vicar retains an air of mild interest bordering on detachment. In an outer room the game-keeper who delivered the hamper is receiving refreshment of bread, cheese, and beer from the bonneted maid. The commentary says the bonneted women by the hamper is also a maid, but the spectacles and more elaborate bonnet of the older woman on the far right suggests she might be a family member rather than the housekeeper.

The *ILN* said *the sending of Christmas gifts, such as may be unpacked from a hamper and placed on a dinner table, is happily still recognised in English society as a proper mode of expressing personal regard.* It then made a particular point about rural hierarchies. *A country clergyman who is, perhaps, by his birth, education, character, and manners, the truest gentleman in his parish, not excepting the squire and the neighbouring peer, may yet without shame accept from the wealthier farmer this seasonal contribution to his larder.* Most Anglican incumbents were Oxford or Cambridge graduates, many had private incomes to supplement their stipends, some had farms attached to their livings, and some whose funds were stretched improved them by turning spare rooms into private schools. Some were magistrates, some were members of the local Poor Law Board of Guardians, and many were trustees of local charities and active managers of church schools. Their range of interest, influence and authority could be extensive, and could actively rival that of the local squire if religious, political and social tensions arose, but usually, if far from universally, the squire and parson considered it best for everyone if they got along reasonably well together.

Rest and be Thankful

From time to time the *ILN* saw fit to view those attending services or involved in church affairs with humour, and notably so at Christmas, but sometimes the humour was blended with more serious allusions. An illustration in the 1874 Christmas Supplement titled *Rest and Be Thankful* by Frederick Barnard (1846-96) showed two chubby children and their aged grandmother asleep during the afternoon service after their Christmas dinner. The title highlights their good fortune in enjoying a plentiful Christmas dinner when so many did not and perhaps hints at their lack of awareness of this. However the accompanying jocular poem sympathised with them, and indeed with other dozing parishioners, rather than with the vicar who seemed out of touch with his congregation (see overleaf).

'Tis good to go to church, for Man's a sinner;
'Tis also good to eat a Christmas dinner;
But if the dinner was a bit too good,
The sermon is not rightly understood,
Dame Margaret fell dozing, very soon,
Till spectacles and Bible, from her lap,
Fell down, and woke her neighbours with a clap;

Frederick Barnard: Rest and Be Thankful – ILN 1874 *Christmas Supplement.*

While both her grandchildren lolled fast asleep,
And still the Vicar's voice its steady drone did keep.

Rest and Be Thankful hints not only at the children's comfortable existence, but also the widowed grandmother's comfort in the children, and perhaps her faith, as she nears her own passing.

The Path to Church

The 1883 Christmas Supplement featured *The Path to Church*, another Christmas picture with an ambiguous title according to the accompanying poem by Byron Webber (1838-1913).

Speaking of the old man clearing the path he says:

Why smiles he not? Why finds he no enjoyment
In labour that wins largesse full and free?
Is it he deems the day for such employment
Is long, long past for one as old as he?

The lad comes next, and he too is less than happy with his lot.

By no means meditative is his servant
That sturdy urchin – whose one wild desire
(I grieve to say the aspiration's fervent)
Is that some injury befal the quire!
He blows the bellows with those blue-cold fingers,
And bans the organist in whispers grim.

Before the days of electric power, and indeed long afterwards in some parishes, church organs were powered by bellows worked laboriously by hand.

Then came the woman and child whose lives are far more comfortable. They clutch their prayer books. They seem not to notice those clearing the path for them.

The comely maiden at the child's touch tarries
To look at Robin, clamorous for crumbs;
His breast almost as ruddy as the berries
That tell the little folk when Christmas comes.

The robin and holly berries made a striking splash of colour and sign of life against the dull grey tombstone and its covering of snow. The woman and child notice this, but the boy and old man do not seem receptive to the scene or its symbolism. Their hearts had hardened. The Druids believed holly was a scared plant and brought fertility and good fortune. As Christianity took hold of the

The Path to Church – ILN *1883*
Christmas Supplement.

country the evergreen holly became a metaphor for eternal life, the sharp leaves represented Christ's Crown of Thorns and the berries symbolised His blood. Multiple stories were associated with robins, and notably their red breasts. Some tales say the red feathers originated when a robin first brought human beings the comfort of fire and his breast was badly singed; other tales say the singeing stemmed from a robin striving to extinguish the fires of Hell on behalf of humans. The robin became the symbol of communication between the human world and the Divine, and therefore was especially welcome at Christmas. The importance of robins and the supernatural to the Victorians is picked up again in Chapter Ten.

Free Seats

In Henry (Hal) Ludlow's illustration *Free Seats* in the 1887 Christmas Supplement a young mother sits lost in thought in church at Christmas. Her prayer book lies on her lap and her arm is around her son. A spiral of holly symbolising eternal life climbs the pillar by her. As their clothing clearly suggests, they are not desperately poor but the title *Free Seats* intimates that the husband is absent, perhaps dead, and they are struggling to maintain

their modest but respectable place in local society. It reminded readers that Christmas could be a particularly difficult time for some people, and that church attendance at this time might heighten sadness as well as bring comfort.

Free Seats had another meaning for Victorian readers. Many pews in churches were reserved for parochial subscribers who could afford the 'pew rent' and display their social status accordingly. Some such pews had doors and names on them to deter others from entering, but the mother and child sit towards the back of the church among the free seats available for poorer worshippers. The accompanying poem summarised conventional Victorian beliefs, while the picture itself belied the message of equality before God preached from Victorian pulpits.

Enter here both rich and poor,
 Come in simple hope and faith;
Leave behind you at the door
 Love of life and fear of death.

Come on this day of days,
 Humbly pray on bended knee.
Sing the fervid song of praise,
 All the seats in heaven are free.

Hal Ludlow: Free Seats – ILN *1887*
Christmas Supplement.

The Front Pew

Another 1887 illustration by Hal Ludlow (1861-1925) concentrated on the front pew often reserved for a local family of distinction. The spiral of holly suggests it might be the same church as in Ludlow's previous illustration. Here, too, a sad looking woman sits with her prayer book on her lap, lost in thought and far away from the Christmas service of celebration. However she is supremely well-dressed as is the stern-faced older man sitting between her and a young girl. The man, it appears, has not even extended the courtesy of allowing the woman to enter the pew before him.

Observers are left to ponder the relationship between the three figures, especially the two most prominent ones, but there are strong suggestions of that frequent theme of Victorian literature, letters and melodramas – the wife trapped in a cold marriage that was little more than a public charade. Neither she, nor perhaps her daughter who is so obviously separated from her in the picture, can easily escape. However, although separation and especially divorce – an extremely expensive enterprise – easily led to social ostracisation and an hitherto 'good' name being irreparably besmirched, by 1882 married women had been accorded some defence against financial and physical abuse by their husbands. The 1839 Custody of Children's Act, the 1857 Matrimonial Causes Act and the 1870 and 1882 Married Women's Property Acts had given women a modicum of protection by allowing them custody of children under the age of seven, transferring divorce cases from ecclesiastical courts to civil ones, identifying just causes, and protecting women from losing their income and property to their husbands upon marriage.

Once again the accompanying poem mouths conventional assumptions while underlining that the Christmas spirit could be entirely absent, even in church.

The village church on Christmas Day
Holds kindly hearts and pleasant faces.
And some are seen to sing and pray
Who seldom go to such places.

But if for only once a year
Their hearts are touched, it makes them better:
And he who feels his conscience clear
Must own himself the season's debtor.

The Victorians remained far from silent on the question of marriage. This illustration was published just a few months before the issue of marriage being little more than a stifling imprisonment for many women blew up in the nation's press. A veritable storm of sympathetic letters – upwards of 27,000 – reached the *Daily Telegraph* when it invited a response to a highly critical article on marriage by the feminist social commentator and novelist, Mona Caird (1854-1932), published in the *Westminster Review.*

Hal Ludlow: The Front Pew – ILN *1887 Christmas Supplement.*

The Squire's Daughter

In December 1885 *The Squire's Daughter* by Marcella Walker highlighted the rural hierarchy. An attractive young woman, clearly from a well-to-do family, holds her prayer book as she enters the church. The *ILN* called her Miss Helen, aged twenty, and *she has a family right to feel herself quite at home anywhere in the village, of which her respected father is the principal owner.* She visits the poorer cottagers regularly, is a Sunday School teacher, and particularly friendly with the rector's wife and daughters. *Her face looks bright, happy and clever, and we cannot doubt that she is everybody's friend and deservedly popular in the neighbourhood. So, as she modestly walks into the church, dressed with an easy but not ungraceful negligence, and forgetting the pretty ornament of a feather in her hat, there is no air of coquetry about her; but her presence is sure to please.*

She seems the model Victorian daughter who in time, the *ILN* asserts, will join the ranks of *British matrons, with every privilege of domestic and social rank to which they were born, and helping to keep up the harmony of mutual trust and goodwill between all classes of the nation.* However *ILN* readers might have noticed that her dress sends out a distinctly personal message about her attitudes and aspirations. Generally speaking, in the mid-1880s bodices were cut to fit the figure closely, were heavily lined and often elaborately boned. Skirts were elaborately pleated and arranged in a narrow bustle which hung down the centre of the back and were often supported by hooped wires inserted into the skirt lining. As with most costly female fashions of the era they were uncomfortable, restricted everyday movement, made breathing difficult and exercise impossible. This young woman, however, is not conforming. A decade or two earlier the artists associated with the Pre-Raphaelite Brotherhood had promoted simpler and more loosely fitted dresses in contrast to the prevailing corsets, bustles and fussy decorations. In 1881 the Rational Dress Society was founded to allow women to be dressed 'healthily, comfortably and beautifully, to seek what conduces to birth, comfort and beauty in our dress as a duty to ourselves and each other.' (Quote: www.glily. com/preraphs.htm). *ILN* readers might have recognised Miss Helen as possessing a rather sensual aesthetic taste in fashion that delighted in relatively simple designs but using luxurious materials. She was in avant-garde company. *ILN* readers may have known that Oscar Wilde, at the height of his fame in the 1880s, was an enthusiastic wearer of velvet jackets and knee breeches, and also a writer and lecturer on aesthetic taste in clothes. And the celebrated illustrator Kate Greenaway often dressed her fictional girls in her Victorian version of looser fitting Regency dresses flowing from Empire waists encircled with a wide waist band tied with a bow at the back and set off with a wide-brimmed straw bonnets. Liberty of London ensured her designs became popular with their more liberally minded wealthy customers.

Marcella Walker: The Squire's Daughter – ILN *19 December 1885.*

The Font & The Flowers

On 22 December 1860 John Leech's illustration *The Font and The Flowers* accompanied a Christmas story. The picture showed several young woman and children, clearly from reasonably well-to-do families, decorating the parish church with two clergymen – the elderly rector and his curate. As it was deemed unlucky to decorate churches and homes beforehand, it must be Christmas Eve. They are using local evergreens – boughs of holly and their berries reminding people of the crown of thorns, crucifixion and resurrection, laurel with its association with victory, the long-lived yew symbolising eternal life, and pines representing the evergreens' triumph over winter darkness. Pine cones and herbs such as rosemary added a pleasant odour to the Christmas Day service. Mistletoe's pagan origins and associations with Druidism meant it was barred from churches, even though most of the other plants had pre-Christian associations too. Ivy, too, was kept out of churches, although ironically many wood carvings in churches included it.

The accompanying story is mischievous. The curate is given a name – Frederick Stanhope. *He is a handsome and agreeable young man, and soon became very popular in the parish.* Earnest in disposition, he is devoted to supporting the sick, poor and dying. He meets the five *blooming daughters* of a widower, *Mr Dymond, a pious banker*, and with much time on their hands their usual pastimes are suddenly extended to include church affairs. For a couple of years the curate had asked a devoted parishioner, the young serious-minded Emily Bexley, for advice and support but as the current discussions for the Christmas decorations took place he found himself overwhelmed by the Dymond sisters as they divided up parts of the church between themselves and pestered him with unnecessary questions. Emily became disappointed in his weakness, especially his acceptance of their entirely excessive floral displays, and said so to him. The overbearing sisters descended upon the church on Christmas Eve, but when Emily arrived she found that the decorations were as they should be, and forgave him. He said she was right, and he was pleased she was pleased. Female superficiality, male weakness, and the redeeming influence of a virtuous woman were all there in this seasonal Victorian morality tale.

Nativity

Over the decades there are remarkably few *ILN* images of the Holy Land or the Nativity. One of these was the pen and ink *Nativity* by the Honourable Mrs Boyle (1825-1916) in December 1863. Usually she signed herself EVB – Eleanor Vere Boyle – to avoid identifying her aristocratic status as the wife of a younger son of the 8th Earl of Cork. She was a much admired artist and book illustrator, notably working with Alfred Tennyson and Hans Christian Anderson. She was strongly influenced by the Pre-Raphaelites, although never tied to their principles, and in this drawing the *ILN* loftily acknowledges she is primarily experimenting with early Italian representations and forms. *The drawing we have engraved is conceived in the true spirit of early Christian poetic and mystic art. Yet it is free from servility of imitation. The crucifixion on the distant Calvary; the Garden of Gethsemane beneath; the star in the east; the nimbi around the various heads; the thorns hedging around the infant Saviour; the angel singing "Peace on earth, goodwill to men!" and accompanying herself on the*

John Leech: The Font and The Flowers – ILN *22 December 1860.*

Eleanor Vere Boyle: Nativity – ILN 19 December 1863.

Italian mandolino, are all naive but poetical anachronisms entirely in the spirit of Early Italian art..... The doves, the roses, lilies, passion-flowers, and other floral emblems are introduced with taste. The whole is admirably composed, and the varied expression and beauty of the faces are quite equal to the elevation of the conception and the delicate unconventionality of the drawing.

An Italian Church at Christmas Time

The *ILN* displayed a condescending British attitude towards overseas Christmas celebrations, not least in scorning cribs. On 27 December 1873 a spectacular illustration of an Italian church at Christmas evoked this commentary:

The Roman Catholic Church in Southern Europe has shown a certain degree of condescension to the less advanced state of intellectual culture among the labouring classes. It has permitted, at the discretion of the parochial clergy, but presumably with the sanction of their bishops, the use of pictures and images not only for the permanent adornment of a sacred edifice, but in a peculiar manner for the visible representation of Bible history upon such occasions as the great festivals of the Christian year. In the judgement of ordinary English Protestants, such an exhibition as that of a set of figures

modelled and arranged, with a landscape background, to display the chief incidents of Our Saviour's life, cannot but seem liable to serious objections, as tending to materialise the popular conceptions of that sublime and most holy theme of the evangelical narrative. It went on to condemn the Passion Play at Oberammergau as mere *artistic entertainment* and concluded that any liberal-minded English visitor to the church it illustrated might look kindly upon the motives of the creators *but he will prefer the Bible classes and Sunday schools of our own country.*

Nativity scenes had spread across Europe from the early thirteenth century when Pope Honorius III (reigned 1216-27) approved St Francis of Assisi's staging of a scene using live animals and a manger to illustrate his preaching. Miracle plays were already popular and along with nativity scenes and religious paintings they helped people understand the Bible when services were in Latin, illiteracy was rife and Bibles scarce. After the English Reformation, and certainly under the seventeenth century Puritans, such representations were suppressed as idolatrous, and natural greenery became the major feature of Christmas decorations in Anglican churches and Nonconformist chapels. The *ILN*'s attitude was a commonplace Protestant one, even in the 1870s, and nativity scenes and cribs crept only slowly into parish churches, largely in the twentieth century.

An Italian Church at Christmas Time – ILN 27 December 1873.

Shepherds Watching Over Their Flocks

On 21 December 1872 a dramatic illustration by William James Webb (1830-1904) featured a group of Syrian shepherds outside Bethlehem watching over their flocks of sheep and goats at night. The *ILN* noted that the moon-lit scene across the valley *might be likened, at first sight, to the privileged shepherds of another Christmas time.* However it is 1872, and the commentary swerved violently away from an angel appearing in their midst with the good news of the birth of Jesus. *But these careless rustic loungers, perhaps of the ordinary condition among their fellow countrymen, do not seem to have heard any extraordinary message of divine grace, or of peace and good will to mankind; for while they repose in easy attitudes, without fear of molestation, one playing on his fife, another inhaling the fumes of his hookah, in a serene stare of*

"kef" (drug induced drowsiness), *their muskets are placed within reach against the rock behind them, to be ready for instant use, if the wild Bedouins of the desert should attack them, to carry off the animals under their charge. Peace and goodwill to all mankind have not yet become the universal and inviolate rule of life in Bethlehem – any more than in London, Paris, Berlin, Rome, New York, and other towns we know.*

Bethlehem, in common with the whole region, fell under Ottoman Turk rule in the thirteenth century, although Christians from Roman Catholic, Greek Orthodox and, much later Protestant Churches, were generally tolerated by the Muslim authorities – even though the Christian sects barely tolerated each other. It remained a poverty-stricken region, Ottoman oppression was easily provoked, and law and order were unreliable commodities – as the *ILN* recorded.

William James Webb: Shepherds Watching over their Flocks – ILN 21 December 1872.

Carving Crosses for Pilgrims at Bethlehem

Nineteenth century Bethlehem possessed few Jews, a sizeable minority of Muslims, and significant Christian communities. In reference to the steadily growing religious and secular tourist trade, the *ILN* said many families from all faiths *gain a livelihood by making beads, crosses, and mother of pearl ornaments, for sale to pilgrims and other visitors.* On 24 December 1870, the *ILN* published William James Webb's picture of a Bethlehem Muslim carving a crucifix with, through the archway behind him, a family scene looking much like the Virgin and Child being visited by the Magi.

Many Victorians would have seen the Virgin and Child as the true inhabitants of Bethlehem, not the Muslim carver, even though the Middle East had long been part of the Ottoman Empire. Most Britons knowledge of the region was limited to the Bible story and to narrow travelogues that largely treated the Holy Land as just that – a sacred land full of Biblical sites to be sought out and revered. Everything else, and notably the complex historical political, religious and demographic contexts, were considered of little significance, and as a result the *ILN*'s illustration would have been particularly thought provoking.

William James Webb: Carving Crosses for Pilgrims at Bethlehem – ILN 24 December 1870.

The Village Choir at Rehearsal

In December 1871 the *ILN* published *The Village Choir at Rehearsal* by Matthew White Ridley (1836-88), with a storyline highlighting the importance of the clergyman's family in motivating villagers to ensure the central Christian theme was to the fore in the Christmas Day service. At this time the Christmas Eve midnight mass was not held in Anglican churches.

Here the *rector's two accomplished daughters* are training the Christmas choir while the church is being decorated and a child sits patiently with a basket of greenery. One sister plays the harmonium sited by a pillar near the pulpit and lectern, while the other grapples with *the set of youthful vocalists chosen out of the Sunday school. A gentle young curate who may be their brother or else the betrothed of one of them, stands beside the instrument and beats time for his sole satisfaction, being in such a position that the movement of his hand can scarcely be observed by any of the performers.*

The sisters were followers of fashion, and at someone's considerable expense they had cast aside the vast circular skirts of previous years for those that fell flat at the front and projected backwards in a bustle. The costly confections of layered petticoats, horsehair cushions, ruffles, pleats and gathers ensured these clergyman's daughters stood out as figures of consequence in the parish.

The commentary thought the *sturdy young rustic* in the smock and gaiters was trying hard, but the well dressed boys from 'better' families were not exerting themselves sufficiently. However the commentary said that if, as it thought likely, they were the sisters' brothers or their friends they would be cajoled into singing properly. The girls on the left were distracted by the singer who dropped her book, and the sister on the harmonium had cast her a *glance of mild remonstrance. But,* insisted the *ILN, the two ladies will succeed, by their patient forbearance of temper, and by their sweetness of manner, combined with strict and firm persistence in requiring due execution of each part, in training this choir to a very tolerable degree of efficiency before Christmas Day.* No doubt they will, as this was the well-established rural hierarchy in operation, ensuring the centrality of respectful worship at Christmas. In many parishes the female members of the clergyman's family were significant figures, not least in supporting the sick, distributing charity, teaching in Sunday Schools, and (unofficially) inspecting the children's art and needlework in the church school.

Matthew White Ridley: The Village Choir at Rehearsal – ILN *16 December 1871.*

The Vicar's Daughter

On 26 December 1891 *The Vicar's Daughter* by George Edward Robertson (1864-1920) presented readers with the epitome of a serious minded young woman dedicated to good works. With her long hair simply drawn back and tied, and dressed plainly in serviceable winter clothing, she is on a Boxing Day mission through the snow-covered village.

Whilst local men of substance generally controlled the purse strings, their wives and daughters customarily ventured forth with goods to give to deserving poor families in the neighbourhood. Just as Victorian society expected the good wife to be both the ruler of the household economy, including the indoor servants, and the pro-active fount of all virtues in holding families and households together, so they often extended these

George Edward Robertson: The Vicar's Daughter – ILN 26 December 1891.

influential roles to the welfare of the wider community. Daughters were brought up to follow in their domestic and charitable footsteps.

Parish clergy were figures of high local standing and local families usually needed no reminding that very often they exercised secular as well as moral authority as charity trustees, Poor Law Guardians, school managers, and sometimes glebe farmers. It was an age when charity was often bestowed only upon the poor thought deserving of it, and drink, profanity, and absence from church could easily transfer one to the undeserving category. No doubt, as the artist suggests in her expression, the vicar's daughter fully appreciated her duty as an Anglican role model and extension of her father's work. Duty was paramount, whether it brought contentment – or a nagging and ultimately frustrating sense of confinement. The artist lets the viewer decide.

The Christmas Anthem

The 1888 Christmas Supplement featured *The Christmas Anthem* by the high profile artist George Jacomb-Hood (1857-1929). The surpliced choir in the chancel is all male, although one of the well-dressed girls sitting below them is adding her voice to the choir, and perhaps the whole congregation, including the priest by the altar, are joining in. By this date many old carols had been rewritten with more obvious Christian themes and many new ones had been compiled ready for church use. A new Christmas service of nine Bible readings telling the Christmas story interspersed with carols was spreading across the country. It had been introduced just eight years earlier, in 1880, by the Right Reverend Edward Benson, the first bishop of Truro, and was held in a temporary wooden building acting as his cathedral until the new Gothic Revival one was completed.

Songs with a Christmas theme have been called carols for many centuries, although some of them with general winter themes probably pre-date Christianity. In the fourteenth century Franciscan friars used a carol sung by people joining hands in a circle, and in 1426 John Awdlay, a Shropshire priest, listed 25 Christmas carols. They may have been sung in homes and alehouses and by wandering 'wassailers' seeking food, drink and money, but almost certainly not in churches. It was not the tradition, and many of the songs were bawdy rather than religious and linked to the popular Lord of Misrule rather than the Nativity. However early forms of *Good Christian men rejoice* and *O come all ye faithful* were extant in the sixteenth century, and religious carols were encouraged as aids to worship in post-Reformation Protestant countries, including England. Martin Luther welcomed them. Possibly *God rest you merry, Gentlemen* (with the comma after *merry*) originates from this era, as do the wassailing songs *We wish you a merry Christmas* and *Deck the halls with boughs of holly.*

When the Puritans dominated England after the execution of Charles I in 1649 the celebration of Christmas ceased by law. Carols survived in secular settings but even after Christmas became legal again after Charles II's restoration in 1660, their popularity was diminished and took time to grow. *While shepherds watched their flocks by night* was written in the seventeenth century and added to an earlier tune, and *Hark the herald angels sing* was written in the eighteenth century by John and Charles Wesley.

It was, though, the nineteenth century that witnessed an outpouring of revised and original carols as Christmas soared in popularity. New choirs and orchestras sought new songs to sing and pieces to play, and in 1822-23 Davies Gilbert published carols he had collected across the country, followed by William Sandys in 1833. These early efforts to preserve and promote carols, and often refine their more earthy and bucolic lines, gave a significant boost to their use in homes and places of worship. The old Cornish carol *The first Noel* was a particular favourite carefully edited and extended. Germany supplied several early carols, with the evocative *Silent night, holy night* composed in 1818, and *O Tannenbaum (O Christmas tree)*, the secular tribute to the evergreen Christmas tree's symbol of constancy, appearing in 1824.

Although secular enjoyment and religious observance were entwined at Christmas, nineteenth century Anglicans and Nonconformists were at pains to ensure the Nativity loomed large in music suitable for incorporation into their acts of worship. Versifiers and composers did not let them down. *O come O come Emmanuel* was translated from the ancient Latin antiphon and popularised as a carol by John Mason Neale in

1851. In the same decade Neale's modernisation led to the success of *Good Christian men rejoice*, whilst his new rendering of *Good King Wenceslas* owed as much to its strident Scandinavian tune as to the murder of the otherwise obscure Christian Duke Vaclav of Bohemia in 935 by his pagan brother. *Once in royal David's city* first appeared in 1848 in Cecil Frances Alexander's instructional *Hymns for Little Children. It came upon a midnight clear, We three kings of Orient are* and *O little town of Bethlehem* were written by different American pastors and crossed the Atlantic soon after their composition in 1849-50, 1857 and 1868 respectively. And in the 1880s *Away in a manger* by an unknown American author (not Martin Luther as previously supposed) also crossed the Atlantic.

George Jacomb–Hood: The Christmas Anthem – ILN 1888 Christmas Supplement.

The Waits (Carol Singers)

In medieval times songs with winter and Christmas themes were sung by groups of musicians called Waits – a term stemming from Christmas Eve being known as 'watchnight' or 'waitnight' when the shepherds were watching over their sheep at the time the angel appeared to them. Originally Waits were official town musicians. They were provided with uniforms and a variety of instruments, and their duties included playing at official functions as well as at festivals, fairs and important weddings. They were licensed to accept money from the public, not least to avoid the charge of begging. The Waits were part of local celebrations that greeted Christmas until the Puritans stepped in, and severely limited their actions. Although they declined in number, officially they did not die away completely until abolished by the 1835 Municipal Corporations Act, but before then and long afterwards any group walking around neighbourhoods at Christmas singing, whether or not for money, tended to be called 'Christmas Waits'. Unlike some Victorian Christmas customs, carol singing had a long, if disrupted, history, as the *ILN* was keen to highlight in several Christmas issues.

On Christmas Day 1847 the *ILN* featured *The Christmas Carol* by Henry George Hine (1811-95). The family of *poor but pious minstrels* are singing *God rest ye merry, gentlemen* and selling one of the many cheap broadsheets printed with carols. A beggar crouches by the well-stocked butcher's shop. Looking up at the singers is a boy in his charity school uniform holding what appears to be his 'school-piece'. This was a sheet of his best handwriting to prove to the trustees and donors that the school was efficient and he was industrious. Perhaps he wrote out the verses of a new carol the group could now sing. The *ILN* added, *We may note that, of late, there has been a revival of taste for the Scriptural Carol. Last year, two or three reprinted*

Henry George Hine: The Christmas Carol – ILN 25 December 1847.

Hablot Knight Browne (Phiz): The Street Carol – ILN 20 December 1851.

collections appeared; one of them illuminated in gold and colour, after the manner of the missal. Perhaps this referred to William Sandys editions of *Christmas Carols: Ancient & Modern* published in 1833.

On 20 December 1851 *The Street Carol* by Phiz (Hablot Knight Browne 1815-82) dramatically reinforced what Christmas meant for many desperate families. Here haunted looking children with their mother are singing carols near the pointedly named Bread Street in the desperate hope of staying alive. It was a striking evocation of the very poor, especially at Christmas, with the walls plastered with a dysfunctional array of advertisements for a concert and music hall, a railway excursion, a pawn shop, food for mothers, a fair to help Polish refugees, and the Grand Metropolitan Cemetery. The image should have been a negation of all things most Victorians associated with Christmas – but of course most Victorians comforted themselves with their share of charitable works together with the rates they paid to provide food and shelter for those admitted to workhouses. And as the prestigious and influential Charity Organisation Society constantly asserted, those with charitable inclinations needed to distinguish between the disreputable poor not meriting support and the worthy deserving a brief and modest helping hand to regain jobs and self-respect.

Carol Singing in Yorkshire

Carol Singing in Yorkshire by John Gilbert (1817-97), published on Christmas Eve in 1864, featured another wintery scene which may or may not have been as pleasant and festive as it appears. Against the emotive background of 'the poor man gathering winter fuel' a large group of local children clothed against the cold as best they could and led by a sturdy lad carrying a fir tree sing to a family watching them from a porch. The family seem to be enjoying the visit, the singers are no doubt expecting a gift in recognition of their efforts, and the family no doubt consider their gift to be an appropriate and comforting seasonal charity – and render them free from obnoxious comments by the singers

Groups of local singers wandering from house to house at Christmas, especially during the Twelve Days of Christmas up to 6th January, were sometimes still referred to as 'Wassailers'. The meaning of Wassail had evolved from the Norse and Old English terms for 'good health' as a form of greeting to its association with the spiced ale used at Christmas festivities and the Wassail bowl that held it. The Victorians looked back, often wistfully, to the imagined well-ordered feudal society in which lords and peasants recognised not only their respective places but also their mutual responsibilities to each other of loyalty, service and protection. The Wassail was a Twelfth Night rite whereby local peasants visited their lord with songs of greeting and loyalty in exchange for which the lord customarily gave them festive food and drink. It seems in later centuries wassailing could descend into *ad hoc* groups paying households potentially frightening rather than friendly visits if the supposedly innocuous songs, such as *We wish you a Merry Christmas,* did not produce the expected figgy pudding and drink, and maybe some coins. As the song says – *we won't go until we get some, so bring some out here.* Not everyone on the receiving end liked wassailing, but it was a custom that proved particularly resilient in the north.

John Gilbert: Carol Singing in Yorkshire – ILN *24 December 1864.*

Henry George Hine: Christmas Carol Singing, by Brighton Fishermen – ILN 1849 Christmas Supplement.

Carol Singing by Brighton Fishermen

The 1849 Christmas Supplement pictured Brighton fishermen singing carols. It was by Henry George Hine (1811-95) whose early life was spent in Brighton. The *ILN* thought the fishermen were *the descendants of a party of Spanish refugees who settled there in the reign of Elizabeth, and were presented by her with certain land, for drying nets and other purposes connected with fishing.... [They] possess characteristics in features and customs not met with amongst other classes in the town, or amidst the peasantry in the neighbourhood. Black eyes and hair, and a clear brown complexion, are common among them, and seem to favour the idea of their southern origin.... Although uncouth in manners, they are industrious and inoffensive, holding but little intercourse, except in the way of business, with the townspeople, whom they* generally designate *"furringers". Their prevailing weakness is for beer, and under its influence become rather uproarious; yet, as they live, make love, marry, and fight among themselves, other classes of the community are not much affected by their peculiarities.* The exception was Christmas when they relaxed *for a time their exclusive prejudices; and forming themselves into groups of carol-singers – or as they termed themselves, "wassailers" – they enter the hotels and private dwelling houses, and there sing their ancient carols.*

In the late 1560s thousands of Calvinist Protestant refugees had fled to England from the Spanish controlled Low Countries to escape persecution by the devoutly Roman Catholic King Philip II and his feared regional governor, the Duke of Alva. Thousands of Huguenots (French Protestants) fled to England in the late 1680s to escape persecution by King Louis XIV.

The end of the Year: Striking Twelve

On 31 December 1883 the illustration *The End of The Year: Striking Twelve* reminded *ILN* readers that New Year could be celebrated in different ways. *The custom observed by many religious congregations, both of the Church of England and of the Wesleyans and Dissenters, is to hold a special meeting for Divine service during the hour before midnight on the last day of the Old Year, so that the actual beginning of the New Year shall be consecrated by prayer, or by the singing of a hymn.* The *ILN* praised the family whose members enjoyed *the genuine sentiment of a heartfelt communion in the highest and holiest affections of which humanity is capable. This appears to be situation of the amiable domestic party, the father, the mother, somewhat younger than her husband, and the daughters by her side, who have been reading, and sometimes exchanging comments or questions, in the most appropriate study, till their common occupation is stopped – or is rather suddenly directed to thinking of the solemnity of the present moment – by the sound of the midnight chimes.* The illustration may well have resonated sympathetically with some *ILN* readers who, even if they did not imitate the family in the picture, were among the millions for whom regular Christian worship was both an ingrained habit from childhood and a source of comfort as adults. The century saw a massive expansion of chapel building by various Nonconformist sects who rivalled the Church of England for members and thereby stimulated an Anglican campaign to restore and enlarge numerous old churches and build hundreds of new ones. The clergy occupied respected positions in most national and local institutions, and every aspect of life from birth to death was covered by services, prayers and Bible readings. In many communities the profession of a faith, and being seen to abide by its moral precepts, was part of being judged respectable and a person of integrity – an important component of 'getting on' in the nineteenth century.

The End of the Year: Striking Twelve – ILN *31 December 1881.*

W.B.Murray: New Year's Eve in Edinburgh – ILN 30 December 1876.

New Year's Eve in Edinburgh

On 30 December 1876 the *ILN* featured the clock striking midnight on New Year's Eve in Edinburgh. It reminded readers that Scotland's Reformation extremism had led to the abolition of saints' days and festivals to celebrate, and therefore New Year's Night took the place of Christmas. The commentary noted the importance of drink: *As soon as twelve o'clock strikes, everyone shakes hands with those around, wishing in each case "a happy new year, and many o'them." Each one drinks some whisky and eats some bun, a kind of plum-cake for the new year, again repeating the same words to all that are present. They then go into the houses of near neighbours, to "first-foot", as it is called, when all this* *is again performed. The younger and more active go off to visit friends, carrying a bottle and some bun. In some cases, often by young men who have sweethearts, they go to the door before twelve, and wait till the hour strikes, so that they may be certain to be the "first-foot" to that particular person. Visiting the houses of friends continues all the next day, when the wishing of each other "a happy new year", and tasting the bottle go on. For about a week , if any friends call, the remark is made that "it is still the new year, and there is a drap in the bottle, so you maun taste."*

65

CHAPTER FIVE

Being Poor at Christmas:
The Moral Imperative

The attitudes of Victorians in possession of ample means towards the sectors of society struggling to make a living, or failing to make a living, were complicated. It remained a society in which the clear Christian precept to have compassion for the poor, and be of help to them, still held true and local charities abounded. Most parishes possessed a variety of funds administered through church or secular trustees offering the poor food, clothing, tools, fuel and sometimes shelter in almshouses. Generally speaking the poor who were seen to live God-fearing and morally upright lives, and were enduring hardship through no fault of their own, were far more likely to receive the benefits than those deemed irresponsible and feckless.

Deep concerns about the poor wracked the Victorians as the industrial age spawned the sprawling urban ghettoes about which horrifying stories were written by newspapers and novelists alike. Few, other than those obliged to live or work there, were keen to venture into these dark corners of the Victorian world, and not surprisingly they became widely condemned as corrupting dens of iniquity, and feared as reservoirs feeding mob violence – which was, in fact, a regular feature of life in this turbulent economic and political age. Compassion for the poor, but also fear of them, made them the centre of attention of charitable societies and philanthropists dedicated to relieving the poverty and cleansing the body and souls of those existing in such foul physical and moral conditions.

Wild fluctuations in both the rural and urban economy reduced many families to temporary and sometimes permanent penury, and so did the ever-present threat of death and crippling diseases such as cholera, typhoid, and tuberculosis striking down the primary wage-earners. And most middle class Victorian families must have been aware that their prosperity, and ways of life, were perilous too. The collapse of businesses and banks, and serious illness, could bring ruin, debt, poverty and despair upon them as much as anyone else. No-one was immune to disaster.

Alongside charity, the centuries-old Poor Law offered relief payments and shelter in assorted local workhouses funded through mandatory rate precepts. In 1834 a dramatic change occurred that reverberated throughout the century. The radical Poor Law Amendment Act did just what its title said – that is, amended the old Poor Law to create large workhouses serving a cluster of surrounding parishes and offering inmates such a rigorously disciplined regime and basic living conditions that only the really desperate would want to seek admission and incur the humiliating label of 'pauper'. It was predicated on the assumption that many of the poor were in lowly circumstances because of their lazy and debauched ways of life, and that work was readily available if only they would go and find it. The fatal flaw in the new Poor Law was that it ignored the dire impact of economic downturns and the inevitable unemployment that followed. The new workhouses became the terror of those hovering on the edge of self-sufficiency, and were heavily criticised for their debasing regimes, and as time past their malign presence altered attitudes towards the desperately poor. On the one hand there remained the suspicion that their numbers included some undeserving of charity and whose fully-merited time in workhouses would shake them out of their disreputable ways, but on the other hand many philanthropists and charities who despised 'pauperisation' increased their efforts to keep the 'respectable' poor well away from them.

A London coal charity queue – ILN *1849 Christmas Supplement.*

Christmas highlighted the ambiguities in Victorian attitudes towards those on the perilous edges of society. The *ILN*'s 1849 Christmas Supplement, for example, claimed that *in no country in the world did open-handed charity scatter her gifts more profusely than in England.* It added, with no doubt a deliberate thread of irony, *With what a zest a man sits down to his Christmas dinner, when he knows he has made some poor family happy by having provided for them on this day – whether it be to subscribe to some coal charity, such as our engraving represents; or only to throw in his mite towards purchasing blankets for the poor, or supplying them once a day with soup. And oh! how little is required to throw the sunshine of happiness around some miserable abode – to scatter smiles where tears and sighs are too often found; and to know that, instead of a sorrowful group, huddling around the all but fireless grate, the little pudding is boiling in the pot, and the small joint turning on its worsted jack.* In tune with those Victorian artists, architects, and clergymen eulogising the Middle Ages as some sort of utopian community enterprise, the *ILN* thought modern times were a mere ghost of such a superior Christian era. *If we sigh for the Christmases of the olden times, it is because Charity then overflowed the land. From the Court, the glad stream ran through abbey and baronial hall, into the lowliest cottage and the humblest shed: even the serf, who was sold like a slave with the soil, shared the feast.*

There were, though, large-scale distributions of food at Christmas that emanated from a traditional sense of *noblesse oblige* by wealthy families. They were part of a widespread recognition by wealthier sections of society of the appalling poverty surrounding them – not just among the unemployed but also in homes where wages were barely at subsistence level. As always charity probably sprung from varying degrees of Christian and human compassion, guilt at the massive gulf in wealth, and fears of violence and revolt by the desperate. And there was always the gratifying sense of dependency and gratitude in the poor, and self-satisfaction in taking part in what was a fashionable humanitarian activity.

On 2 January 1847 the *ILN* described Queen Victoria's family Christmas at Windsor Castle. The centre-piece for the thirty-one people was *a splendid baron of beef cut from the carcass of a Highland heifer.* It weighed 256 pounds, occupied twelve hours in roasting and was served cold at the royal table. *There were also on the banquet table several turkeys, Cochin China pullets, and other descriptions of poultry, bred and fattened at the royal aviary at Home Park.* There was also an illustration of some of the 250 poor from Windsor receiving royal gifts of cold meat, bread, plum pudding and beer.

At Christmas the the *ILN* often covered the special efforts of London missions, all of which relied upon donations. The need was large. On 31 December 1887, for example, it reported the previous week's variety of initiatives catering for thousands of people. The East London Mission distributed the ingredients for hundreds of Christmas dinners; the actress Edith Woodworth and the Ragged School Union provided Christmas dinner, presents and an entertainment for a thousand poor children from families connected with London's theatres; the Bloomsbury Chapel Mission provided 350 families with Christmas dinner in its hall; Mrs Emily Fair and the Free Unsectarian Mission in Highbury gave 600 families the ingredients for Christmas dinners; the Hare-court Chapel in Canonbury provided 160 poor families with Christmas provisions, and gave 6d to each of the 400-500 children in local workhouses; Mr A.A. Johnston organised Christmas dinners for 250 poor families (a thousand people) in Croydon's Skating Rink Hall; the Field Lane Refuges and Ragged Schools gave meals to 700 destitute men and women; and the South London Committee of the 'Pinch of Poverty' Relief Fund provided dinners for 400 poor families without employment and gave fifty pairs of boots to the worst cases. The *ILN* noted that *the distribution of Christmas gifts to the poor was continued on Boxing Day at various metropolitan institutions.*

Christmas at the Refuge for the Destitute

There are many pictures of such missions. On 30 December 1843, the *ILN* printed two pictures and an up-beat report on Christmas at the Refuge for the Destitute & Homeless Poor in Islington's Whitecross Street. Founded in 1820 by London businessmen to offer food and overnight shelter during the winter months to migrant families arriving in the city, it was housed in a donated warehouse and was supported *by the contributions of the affluent and, and, and well merits the patronage of all who enjoy the luxury of doing good.* It catered for 650 people a night, with men in one vast room and women and children in another. Each person was given warm water, soap and a towel with which to wash on arrival, half a pound of bread to eat, and straw – clean it was emphasised – to sleep on the floor. A fire burned all night, the rooms were well ventilated to minimise infection, and fresh water was readily available – something of a luxury at that time. A clergyman and a doctor visited nightly. Christmas, though, was a little different. *At one o'clock on Christmas Day each individual was provided with a pound of cake, bread and cheese, and beer, in the presence of Mr William Edwards, chairman of the institution.* And in the evening the women and children were given more cake and some coffee.

Gifts to the poor at Windsor Castle – ILN *2 January 1847.*

Refuge for the Destitute: the Female Ward – ILN 30 December 1843.

Refuge for the Destitute: the Male Ward – ILN 30 December 1843.

Clare Market Ragged School – ILN 25 December 1869.

Clare Market Ragged School

In 1869 the *ILN* appeared on Christmas Day and one poignant illustration showed children of the Clare Market Ragged Schools in St Clement Danes having their weekly evening dinner of pease-porridge. Around 300 children attended the weekday, evening and Sunday classes, and half the children had a meal each Tuesday, and half each Thursday. *When the children are there assembled, the boys on one side and the girls on the other, everyone holding his or her basin, cup, jug, mug, or gallipot fetched in haste from their wretched homes to receive the warm mess of nourishing food, it is a lively place enough.* They came from the maze of narrow streets between the Strand and the corner of Lincoln's Inn Fields, nor far from the offices of the *Illustrated London News*. Without the ragged schools, asserted the *ILN*, all they knew was *hunger, thirst, cold and filthy homes...Born of thieves, reared by thieves, all that they know of good is to be successful in their raids upon society, and the only evil to be detected.* (Quote: *ILN* 22 December 1855) The local clergy and members of the mission provided teachers for the classes, and members of the children's families were offered the support of a Penny Bank, a Lending Library, Penny Readings, Mothers' Meetings and a Sick & Relief Provident Society.

The 1869 article said *Yesterday, being Christmas Eve, there was a special treat, instead of the ordinary pease-porridge dinner; and there will be a good supper of meat and pudding on Monday evening next* (New Year); *for which cause, and for many other reasons, needing few additional words of persuasion, we commend the Clare Market works of beneficence to those who have a little money to spare for deeds of* human kindness at this appropriate season. No doubt roast beef, potatoes, bread and ale were followed by spicy plum pudding, all paid for by well-wishers. The ingredients for an earlier Ragged School Christmas dinner for 300 children included *190 lb. of fine roast beef, 12 plum puddings of 16 and 18 lb each, 2 cwt of best potatoes, 9 gallons of table ale, bread &c. The puddings were comprised of 77 lb of plums, 25 lb of currants, 7 lb of candied peel, 1 gallon of milk, 1½ lb of spice, 10 quarterns of flour, 8 lb of bread, 240 eggs, and 24 lb of suet.* (Quote: *ILN* 6 January 1849) Grace was said at the beginning, the National Anthem sung at the end, thanks were given to the donors, and a talk told the children of the opportunities open to them through a sound education and living God-fearing lives.

There were many Ragged Schools across the nation's great cities. They sought to attract the children of the very poor to a basic education in literacy, numeracy, morality, Christianity and practical skills likely to strengthen them against the physical and moral dangers pervading the slums, help them get a job and enhance their self-respect. Clothing, and notably boots, were provided for the most desperate cases. The classes were held in the day, in the evening, and on Sundays, and children attended when their work load, domestic duties, health and strength allowed. The influential reformer, the 7th Earl of Shaftesbury (1801-85), was instrumental in bringing Ragged Schools together in the Ragged School Union to promote their work in bringing a degree of care and training to those utterly bereft of life's basic necessities and means of improvement.

The Christmas Dole

On 20 December 1856 an engraving of *The Christmas Dole* by the successful landscape painter George Dodgson (1811-80) appeared in the *ILN*. A group of supplicants has gathered in the snow beneath the forbidding hilltop baronial hall. The accompanying article, by a different hand, explored the scene from the perspective of Mr Bumble, the self-important parish beadle in *Oliver Twist*. He noted *an able-bodied pauper, just at the gate, touching his hat. I suppose he is telling his pitiful story, nine ounces of lies to one of truth, as we tell the paupers that come bothering us ... The only thing about the picture that I can at all approve of is that the lower orders are made to keep their distance, and not allowed* to come up to the house to annoy their betters. It's better to keep them away for you give paupers an inch they'll take an ell (the length of the elbow and hand), *and some of the women and children might insinuate themselves in at the door, under pretence of thanking the ladies or the like (not that they have any real thankfulness in them, far from it), and then they are mighty handy with their fingers.* Bumble is displeased that the picture does not show the paupers as suitably miserable. Instead, he bemoans, they are *receiving their Dole and going off to enjoy their Christmas,* and the owner of the mansion is *actually pleased to have the opportunity of making them happy.* No doubt the *ILN*'s readers recognised the all-too-common attitudes beneath the heavy humour.

George Dodgson: The Christmas Dole – ILN 20 December 1856.

The Cottage & The Hall

On 24 December 1859 two illustrations, *Christmas: the Cottage Door* by Miles Birkett Foster (1825-99) and *Christmas: the Hall Door* by Samuel Read (1815-83) were accompanied by a comforting poem (at least to many middle-class readers) by Cuthbert Bede. This was the doubly Saxon *nom de plume* of the Reverend Edward Bradley (1827-89), a Lincolnshire clergyman and prolific writer of novels, articles and verse. St Cuthbert (c634-687) was a monk and bishop at Lindisfarne, and Bede (c672-735) a monk, writer and teacher at Jarrow.

Birkett Foster showed a wife and three children welcoming home their father who is carrying a cloth covered basket to their thatched cottage, and Samuel Read pictured costumed guests being welcomed by flaming torches to a brightly lit mansion. Bede's poem highlighted not the multiple differences but the joyful similarities between the two Christmas scenes, and the equality the rich and poor possess in God's eyes – if not those of carefully stratified Victorian society. Christmas, he was suggesting, is a glimpse into heaven. It has four verses, and last two read:

The light that streams through lordly panes,
 And makes the painted windows burn,
Is answer'd back from lowly lanes,
 Where children hail their sire's return.
The wild bells ring with Christmas mirth,
 And tell their tale of holy lore, –
Glory on High, goodwill on Earth, –
 Alike at Hall and Cottage door

Ay! this the key-note Christmas gives
 To cheer us through the twelvemonth long,
And tune the burden of our lives
 To echo back the angels' song.
Oh! may we join the glorious band
 When, earthly joys and struggles o'er,
Dwellers in Hall and cot shall stand
 On equal terms at Heaven's door.

Miles Birkett Foster: Christmas: the Cottage Door – ILN 24 December 1859.

Samuel Read: Christmas: the Hall Door – ILN 24 December 1859.

Distress in the North

Two editions of the *ILN* – on 20 and 27 December 1862 – straddled Christmas Day, and both eulogised voluntary efforts to help the unemployed cotton workers in the North of England. They were the helpless victims of, first, over-production when unsold goods accumulated in warehouses and led to reduced hours of work, and then the severe disruption of supplies of raw cotton during the American Civil War of 1861 to 1865 caused by the blockade of southern Confederate ports by their northern Union opponents.

On 20 December 1862 the *ILN* reported that 448,955 people were dependent on parochial aid or the charities specially convened to raise funds and distribute food and clothing. A picture and article highlighted the generosity of the railway and canal director, John Chapman (1810-77), MP for Great Grimsby, in providing provisions each Tuesday and Friday for over 700 families a week at his house in Mottram, near Manchester.

Operatives from the cotton mills of Broadbottom, Stockport, Hatfield and other places are continually paying visits to and enjoying the beneficence of this gentleman. The vast amount of self-sacrificing charity ... makes one's heart leap with joy in the midst of its sorrow for the distressed operatives.

On 27 December another illustration and article concentrated upon Manchester's Gaythorn Cooking Depot and Dining Rooms hurriedly created in Messrs Fearnley's Mill, largely on the initiative of John Pender (later Sir John: 1816-96) who had textile factories and warehouses in the city and Scotland. *Considering the completeness, cleanliness and order of the establishment, it is remarkable that it should have been organised and opened in the short period of twenty-one days.* The *ILN* did not add that thousands of desperate families left the region in search of work, thousands more laboured on huge public projects (mainly roads but also public parks) and thousands subjected themselves to the Poor Law before a semblance of normality returned after the American Civil War ended.

Cotton workers waiting for breakfast in Mr Chapman's yard – ILN 20 December 1862.

Manchester's Gaythorn Cooking Depot & Dining Rooms – ILN 27 December 1862.

Light & Shadow

Not long before Christmas in 1875 the *ILN* featured the evocative painting *Light & Shadow* by Matthew White Ridley (1837-88), and a poem of the same name by J.L. This is possibly John Latey (1808-91) who was editor of the *ILN* from 1858 until 1890, or maybe his son, also John Latey (1842-1902), a journalist and contributor to the *ILN*.

On a cold snowy night a young mother with a child tries to rest on steps outside a town house where through a nearby window a party can be seen taking place. The wall and especially the railings bear down upon her, accentuating her isolation. The mother and child are in the vestiges of fine clothes as though recently she has known far better times, and the poem lays bare the harsh Victorian truth that joy can be quickly followed by sorrow just as summer turns to winter, and days from light to dark. And ominously it notes that the sorrows may or may not be of our own making. We do not know why the mother and child are on the streets. Has her husband, or perhaps her lover, died or deserted her? Has she been ejected from her home for some offence? And we do not know whether the party-goers have noticed her, or care.

The mawkish poem is full of doubtful religious points and moral warnings. The first three verses dwell on the eternal sequence of day and night, the seasons, the cycle of life and death, and the essentially human lot of laughter and tears, triumph and disaster. The final three verses, seen below, link the human transition between happiness and misery to the actions humans take and suggest that this is part of God's plan for his creation.

*Matthew White Ridley: Light &
Shadow – ILN 15 December 1875.*

Light and shadow closely mingle
  In the gracious scheme divine;
Joy and sorrow come not single,
  But join hands and intertwine;
Now with bliss our beings tingle,
  Now in grief we lie supine.

If we kept life as we take it,
  With its sweet vicissitude!
But our crimes and errors make it
  Oft a nest of scorpion brood;
Knowing good, we yet forsake it,
  Well content with swinish food.

Did we strive to lighten sorrow,
  Give the wronged all righteous aid,
Then new light our life would borrow,
  And a host of wrongs be laid;
Then would dawn each coming morrow
  Fairer on a world new made.

The Poor Seamstress on Christmas Morning

On 22 December 1877 an illustration entitled *The Poor Seamstress on Christmas Morning* provided the *ILN* with an opportunity to reflect upon the circumstances that had reduced this young woman, and by implication many thousands of others, to such perilous circumstances. The article hoped she would claim *the respectful sympathy of those in happier or easier circumstances,* not least because she seems to be reading the Bible and recollecting the day's *hallowed and gracious associations.* It hoped her sprigs of holly would be accompanied by *some little addition to her scanty repast.*

The *ILN* was, no doubt, fully aware that seamstresses were often in the grip of exploitative workshop owners or middlemen, and stories abounded that many had to supplement their pitiful wages with prostitution. The *ILN* left no stone unturned in imagining her sad past, and miserable future. *It is touching, indeed, to reflect that she may have left or lost a home of her childhood ... Her lot in life, whether by unavoidable misfortune, by the cruelty and injustice of others, or by such error of conduct on her own part as is seldom forgiven to a woman, has become a sad and hard lot indeed, and it is as much as we can hope for her now that she should merely be able to earn her bread.* Interestingly the seamstress's room is well fitted out with furniture, bedding, crockery and food for someone supposed to be desperately poor. The *ILN* tantalised its readers: is this young woman striving steadfastly to save herself or sadly sliding into utter degradation? It is a theme endlessly repeated in Victorian publications, possibly because it was endlessly enjoyed by 'shocked' readers.

The Poor Seamstress on Christmas Morning – ILN 22 December 1877.

William Heysham Overend: Gypsy Life – ILN 13 December 1879.

Gypsy Life

Approaching Christmas 1879 the *ILN* published a strikingly detailed picture by William Heysham Overend (1851-98) of four young gypsies in their traditionally styled van parked near Latimer Road in Notting Hill. They are poor but look well, the furniture and fittings are old but remain serviceable, and utilising the fire and bedding they are keeping warm. Gypsies were seen by Victorians as racially and culturally different and, living outside accepted social norms, they were feared as feral, unpredictable and unsettling, and never wanted nearby. At the same time, though, they held a fascination as exotic and other-worldly, as epitomised by artists frequent portrayals of wild, dark-eyed, seductive young gypsy women, and stories involving gypsies as practitioners of necromancy, casters of spells and abductors of children. Perhaps Overend's portrayal hints at all these perceptions.

The commentary possessed little Christmas cheer. It adopted a high moral tone while highlighting the stark social contrasts and clearly saw gypsies as a disturbing affront to civilisation. Incongruously, it asserted, the gypsies are *squatting within an hour's walk of the Royal palaces and of the luxuriant town mansions of our nobility and opulent classes, to the very west of the fashionable West End, beyond the gentility of Bayswater and Whiteley's avenue of universal shopping. It is a curious spectacle in that situation, and might suggest a few serious reflections upon social contrasts at the centre and capital of the mighty British nation, which takes upon itself the correction of every savage tribe in South and West Africa and Central Asia.* By condemning the overcrowding of gypsy vans it reflected the widespread suspicion of immorality in such situations, and bemoaned the accumulation of gypsy encampments defacing the capital at Christmas time and over the winter. It thought the Home Office, f*or the sake of public health and good order, should order local authorities to tackle the eccentricities of gypsy life.* It forgot to add that the gypsies were a vital source of seasonal labour on the farms of the south-east and in the hop fields of Kent.

New Year's Eve at St Giles's Workhouse

In January 1884 the *ILN* published a page of assorted drawings by Harry Furniss (1854-1925) depicting New Year's Eve at St Giles's Workhouse in Bloomsbury, London. Such cartoon sequences were common in the *ILN*, and treated people and events with satirical humour ranging from gentle and sympathetic, as here, to piercing and painful. Until recently St Giles's Workhouse, housing up to 900 paupers, had had an unenviable reputation. In July 1865 *The Lancet* condemned nearly everything about its infirmary – the dirty, lice-ridden bedding, the untrained nurses who themselves were paupers, the coal dust permeating every ward, and the inadequate heating and ventilation. By the 1880s, however, new buildings, regulations and staff, notably the energetic new Master, Mr Ellis, had contributed to great improvements.

The entertainment was organised by Mr Ellis and directed by John Maclean, *a veteran comedian*. All of the named performers were regular theatre and music hall performers. Around 550 of the 834 inmates – the others were too ill or infirm to attend – sat beneath a stage decorated in red bands and evergreens. The women wore white caps, grey shawls and dresses of blue workhouse check: the men were dressed in the ubiquitous loose jackets and corduroy trousers seen in most workhouses.

It seems the entertainment, a typical late Victorian medley of popular songs, recitations and recitals, was a great success. *How they chuckled at the woes of 'Poor Suzian' sung with ironical pathos by Mr. Fred Rogers, and listened with rapt attention when Miss Annie Hughes recited the thrilling story of 'The Life-Boat'. How they enjoyed Mr. George Buckland's unctuous humour as he gave his own version of the history of William Tell and roared at the quaint antics indulged in by Mr. T. as the accompaniment to the ditty 'I am so volatile'... .A hushed attention accompanied the sentimental ballads given by Miss Chetwynd, Miss Bussell, Mr. J.F. Fitzgerald and Mr. George Fox. The old heads waggled to and fro with enjoyment during the pianoforte and violin solos by Messrs Jones and Arnold, and when Mr. Fred Ward gave Linley's touching ballad of 'The Irish Emigrant' many of the old women were to be seen with tears rolling down their cheeks.*

Poor Suzian – The Reverie of Poor Susan by William Wordsworth (1770-1850) is about a country girl working in London who is reminded of her home village by hearing a thrush singing in the early morning.

The Lifeboat – This may refer to William McGonagall's poem celebrating Grace Darling's heroic rescue of survivors from a ship wrecked in a storm on the Farne Islands in 1838. In 1884 Annie Hughes (1869-1954) was already a celebrated child actress with a long career ahead of her.

I am so volatile – This was a popular song originally part of a comic sketch from the 1870s called *The Silver Wedding* by the composer, singer and actor George Grossmith (1847-1912).

The Irish Emigrant – The lyric by Helen Blackwood, Lady Dufferin (1807-67), is about a young Irishman visiting his beloved wife's grave just before he emigrates.

Harry Furniss: New Year's Eve at St Giles's Workhouse – ILN 12 January 1884.

Alfred Robert Quinton: Ruined – ILN 1888 Christmas Supplement.

Ruined

As we have seen, Christmas did not deter the *ILN* from including cautionary tales – indeed it delighted in doing so at the festive season. In 1888 the Christmas Supplement included the painting *Ruined* by the prolific countryside artist Alfred Robert Quinton (1853-1934). The once impressive (and fictional) Tudor mansion was surrendering to the weather and undergrowth because its last owner, Squire Hawthorne, had cravenly surrendered his prestige and patrimony to gambling. The poem, by an unknown hand, exudes contempt for the man whose culpable neglect of his responsibilities threatened not only his family but also the well-being of local people – ranging from his tenant farmers to his domestic servants – who to a significant extent depended upon his careful stewardship of his landed estate.

*Sure, none who knew it in its prime would recognise
The Grange:*
Ten years ago I saw the place – and now, O what a change!
For then a fair and gracious dame, with girls, the county's boast,
And stalwart lads, a genial band, were clustered round our host;
Then on their closely-shaven lawn, throughout the summer day,
Was gathered many a jocund throng, in sports and pastimes gay;

For thither flocked, in eager haste, the neighbours all around,
By ties of cordial friendship knit, as in one family bound.

But soon a change came o'er the scene – clouds gathered in a trice;
For how can any homer survive the rattle of the dice?
Our host, alas! poor, simple man, plunged heavily in play,
And quickly squandered all his wealthy in gambling dens away:
So, Squire Hawthorne, who erewhile looked all men in the face,
Slunk from his family and friends, to hide his dire disgrace:
The Grange no longer holds its head in patrimonial pride,
And his sweet wife and children dear are scattered far and wide.

Many social commentators thought gambling was the scourge of the upper classes, but all attempts to curtail it failed – including the Nonconformist inspired National Anti-Gambling League founded in 1890. The exclusive clubs that grew out of the Georgian coffee houses such as White's, Brooke's, Almack's and, later, Crockford's, were as much concerned with drinking and gambling as with politics. Avoiding all legal restrictions, wealthy members wagered not just on card games, the throw of the dice, and horses races, but on anything that came into their heads.

Casual Relief

Casual Relief by Charles Trevor Garland (1855-1906) was included in the 1890 Christmas Supplement. The double meaning of the title given to this picture of a girl from a well-to-do family feeding hungry birds by an open window would be instantly apparent to readers of the *ILN*. She is well-dressed, complete with bonnet and scarf, and perhaps idly amusing herself for a few minutes before going out in the snow. Her pet dog sits obediently beside her, but staring with latent hostility at the hungry birds.

Casual Relief was also the term applied to the help given to those termed 'vagrants' who appeared each night at the door of workhouses in the hope of admittance. They were at the opposite end of the social spectrum to the girl in the illustration. Vagrants were mainly men, but also included a minority of women and children, who were without visible means of support who wandered the country and were given basic food and shelter overnight in return for work the following morning – in the case of men, chopping wood for fuel or breaking stones for road ballast. There were some avidly disliked 'professional tramps' among them, but many were the unemployed forced to leave their home areas to seek work in times of great hardship – such as the Lancashire textile slump of the early 1860s. Most Poor Law authorities had some sympathy with genuine seekers of work but hoped they would quickly move on and not become a drain on local ratepayers. No doubt, like the birds fed by the little girl, they would soon be forgotten.

Charles Trevor Garland: Casual Relief – ILN 1890 Christmas Supplement.

Moving on

On 20 December 1873 a picture of a damp foggy night in St James's Park in London showed a policeman ejecting rough sleepers from its benches. Those being moved on included a mother with two young children amidst the groups of men clustered around the trees. The accompanying commentary seems to display little sympathy with the vagrants, but perhaps readers discerned a deliberate over-playing of the argument.

Disingenuously, it stated: *As we sit by the warm fireside or at the plentiful table, in the evening of one of those days about Christmas-time, we do not much like to think of anybody wanting to stay all night upon a damp bench under the dripping boughs of the trees, now bared of their foliage in St. James's Park. Yet there are such desolate and destitute persons loitering there, within a bowshot of the Queen's palace, and it is the duty of a policeman to bid them 'move them on'; for serious dangers to the peace and safety of her Majesty's liege subjects might be feared if people of every vagrant class were allowed to lurk in any numbers among the Westminster groves and to remain long after dark.*

With heavy humour, the *ILN* comforted readers by reminding them that even at Christmas *The casual wards of the several workhouses, indeed, are open for them till a certain hour; and the lock-up cells of the police stations, when one has qualified oneself for admission at any time by committing a slight offence, will be available at any time of the night. But the regular British vagrant would rather lie on the grass, soaked by the rain, than submit to the strict order of workhouse or prison.* By all accounts, the regimes of Victorian prisons and workhouses were viewed with equal horror by the poor.

L. Wagner: Moving On – ILN 20 December 1873.

The Christmas Dinner given to the Manchester Newsboys – ILN 3 January 1874.

The Christmas Dinner given to the Manchester Newboys

Despite the desperately slow accumulation of laws restricting children's employment, in the 1870s thousands of children still worked long hours. Whether at school or not, many boys and some girls provided a valuable supplement to the family income by delivering or selling daily newspapers. With the stamp duty abolished in 1855, newspapers were soaring in number and popularity. It was becoming a highly competitive market that relied upon rapid printing, bundling up and rail transport, and then rapid delivery to agents, shops, subscribers and street stands. The *Times* and *Observer* had been established since 1785 and 1791 respectively, the *Daily Telegraph* was launched in 1855, and in that year the *Manchester Guardian* went from weekly to daily. Thousands of children assisted every stage of the daily routine, and many were rowdy hawkers of copies on busy streets as the numbers sold counted towards their earnings. Often there were evening editions to deliver and sell. Hours were long, and the work hard.

The *ILN* thought this trend in juvenile employment was highly commendable and welcomed its spread from London to the provinces. On 3 January 1874 it pictured 400 children sitting down to Christmas dinner provided by the proprietors

of the *Manchester Evening News*, founded in 1868 and recently purchased by the *Manchester Guardian*. It was the second such occasion. The *ILN* said the newspaper had *always shown a kindly interest in the welfare of its little customers*, and *boys and girls who were formerly sent out to beg, or perhaps to do worse, now have the opportunity to earn a few shillings a week.*

The dinner was held at the impressive Royal Exchange Restaurant, and was attended by the Bishop of Manchester, the mayors of Manchester and Salford, David Chadwick (a Manchester businessman and Liberal MP for Macclesfield), and *a great number of ladies and gentlemen*. Not surprisingly publicity was as high on the agenda as good-will. And not surprisingly *The children were at first a little awed at the sight of the visitors, but soon grew uproariously merry.* The bishop said grace, a beef dinner and plum pudding were eagerly consumed, during which *the band of the 1st Manchester Rifles played a selection of popular music, and whenever an air struck their fancy the children joined in, keeping excellent time and tune.* A boy of colour sits at bottom right.

The *ILN* said that a show of hands suggested that many of the 400 children were attending day school as *a fair proportion of them knew something of two, at least, of the "three R's"* (reading, writing and arithmetic) although it did not specify which two.

Frans Huard: The Pleasures of Hope – ILN 23 December 1876.

By 1874 the School Boards created by the 1870 Education Act were gradually 'filling the gaps' in the nation's scattered elementary school provision. The gaps in Manchester's provision were undoubtedly significant as 40 large new elementary schools were built in the rapidly expanding city over the next thirty years. However attendance was not compulsory until the 1876 Education Act required parents to ensure their children received 'an efficient education', and the 1880 Act enforced attendance up the age of ten. In 1893 the leaving age was raised to 11. Despite growing concern about the welfare of children working several hours before and after their school day the work of the early morning and evening 'newspaper-boys' had many decades to run.

The Pleasures of Hope

On 23 December 1876 the *ILN* published an engraving of Frans Huard's painting *The Pleasures of Hope* which once highlighted the degree to which the poor were subject to the whims of the wealthy when it came to charity. The commentary says, *the elder lad, the poor, ragged Savoyard, with his fiddle capable of indefinite squeaking, has probably not seen this English dainty before, and views it with an eye of critical curiosity that half beguiles him of downright hunger. The little fellow with the slung satchel has a determined air of resolve to attack the tempting dish, if he could, and if he dared.*

The commentary sees any donor of money to purchase the Christmas pudding as playing *a kindly practical joke* on the boys. Essentially the rich are playing with poor by ignoring or indulging them as the mood takes them. There was little pity for the boys but admiration for the young woman *who has just come out of Robinson's drapery shop, with a few pieces of small change from the counter still in her hand, while she opens the morocco leather portemonnaie* (purse) *to put her money in. Ah! the boys are in rare luck, for her kind glance has fallen upon them, and she is thinking what fun it would be to see them enjoy a little bit of Christmas cheer. It is not every girl or young woman of her rank and breeding that would have the courage to play such a trick.*

CHAPTER SIX

Those Not At Home For Christmas: Worlds Away

Although many *ILN* illustrations promoted the idea that Christmas was essentially a family affair, many Victorian families had splintered into far-flung units. Travel by steam powered locomotives and ships was getting much easier, sons left home to pursue advancement wherever their careers choices took them, and daughters who married followed their husbands. Modern industries and evolving technologies, and the maintenance and exploitation of the expanding Empire, were creating a host of new career opportunities, and these led many men, and their wives and families, far from their original homes. Such migration had always occurred but it surged as

the hectic nineteenth century marched on. And not surprisingly the *ILN* chose its festive issues to highlight what it took to be the thoughts of those away from home at Christmas. The *ILN* itself did not envisage Christmas as much of a holiday for its workers, with issues published on Christmas Eve and Christmas Day as the calendar dictated.

Christmas in Australia

In December 1870 and again in December 1873 the *ILN* published pictures of English and Scottish gold diggers in Australia at Christmas. They were drawn by the well-known artist William Ralston

William Ralston: Christmas in Australia 'Home Sweet Home' – ILN 24 December 1870.

(1841-1911) who had spent several months as a young prospector in Victoria in 1859, although he was one of the many who failed to make his fortune there. Possibly the 1870s illustrations came from earlier sketches he had made on site. They showed groups of prospectors sleeping, chatting, eating and drinking within and outside their makeshift tents and huts. The occasional aborigine looks on or is engaged as a guide. The men look pensive and tired rather than joyful, but they still remember Christmas and home.

The lure of Australian gold had attracted tens of thousands of prospectors alongside William Ralston, notably in Victoria. Loaded down with a tent, blankets, tools, a pot for food, and some tea, sugar and flour, they rode or trudged from the ports to the digging fields, paid a licence fee, and set to work panning, surface digging or mining in spare spaces. Life was rough, and virtually lawless slum tent-cities proliferated. Itinerant dealers sold food and drink at exorbitant prices, and in many gold fields shanty towns started to emerge with saloons, brothels, trading posts and assay offices. The dangers of disease, theft, violence and abject failure were offset by the sight and celebration of the success of the relatively few. Their stories in turn fuelled thoughts of emigration and future riches in many restless young men in Britain's towns and villages.

Over the decades the population of Australia soared, vast quantities of gold were found and numerous new sources were identified across the huge continent. Gradually the Wild West attributes of the early gold fields were tamed by legislation, stronger policing, more responsible business systems and, in the richer gold fields, permanent townships with elected councils and public services. In the 1870s, when the *ILN*'s illustrations appeared, the Wild West lives of prospectors had already assumed a nostalgic mantle of exciting manly adventure, even though working in the newly discovered diggings in Western Australia remained primitive, and dangerous.

Christmas in the New World

On Christmas Eve 1887 readers could gaze in wonder, and perhaps sympathy, at a winter scene in the Canadian outback. It was the work of Richard Caton Woodville (1856-1927) whose fame rested largely on his first-hand accounts and paintings of overseas battles.

With some justification the *ILN* considered the vast northern Canadian forests were fit only for hardy adventurers, whom it blandly judged to be little more than sad exiles from the Old World. By the 1880s Christmas had become such a festival of family and domesticity that it was assumed anyone absent from such a gathering would be full of regrets. *The backwoodsman is far removed from the comforts of home, and scantily provided with the means of shelter.... Wrapped in his thick blanket, with his fur cap pulled over his ears, trying to warm his benumbed feet at a fire of sticks, he smokes the pipe of patience, while hearing in fancy the merry church bells of his native village in the dear old country, and seeing in imagination the friends of his youth, assembled with kindly Christmas greetings, looking forward to the plentiful feast, the social talk, the jests and games and customary pleasures, the homely and neighbourly company he no longer shares.* The contrast is made crystal clear. *Then, hungry as he feels, about to turn out a remaining handful of musty flour to make his "damper" cake, he is relieved by the approach of his attendant Indian huntsman, well-clad in buckskin mantle and loose trousers wrought by the squaws, armed with a double-barrelled flint-gun and broad dirk. The faithful huntsman has brought a hare has caught and killed. Let the hare be cooked and eaten, though without currant-jelly, and it will be a tolerable Christmas dish.*

In 1867 the Province of Canada (Ontario and Quebec), Nova Scotia and New Brunswick had come together in the Confederation of Canada, and gradually other territories joined it – Hudson's Bay in 1868, North West Territories in 1870, British Columbia in 1871 and Yukon in 1898. Constant tension existed between the early British and French settlers, and from the 1840s the numerous Irish emigrants escaping famine displayed little affection for the British they encountered. By the mid nineteenth century the native Indians (latterly termed the First Nations) were already deemed 'non-citizens', and a policy of forced assimilation was underway that banned their traditional dress and ceremonies, pressurised them to convert to Christianity, and sent their children away to Church-run residential schools dedicated to eradicating their culture.

Richard Caton Woodville: Christmas in the New World – ILN 24 December 1887.

Making a Christmas Pudding in China – ILN 20 December 1873.

Making a Christmas Pudding in China

After China had been obliged by British victory in the wars of 1839-42 and 1856-60 to legalise the opium trade, open up ports to European trade, and cede Hong Kong and Kowloon to Great Britain, there was an influx of British officials, merchants, missionaries and military personnel. Despite China's continued loathing of British interference in its affairs, many Chinese found advantageous employment with British households, firms and institutions. On 20 December 1873, just over a decade later, *ILN* readers were presented with the strange image of an Englishman teaching a group of Chinese servants how to make a Christmas pudding.

A convoluted commentary created the story of a coterie of Englishmen in China seeking to recreate an English Christmas but without the skills of doing so until one colleague admitted he possessed a plum pudding recipe. With heavy humour, the *ILN* eulogised him as Tennyson's 'fair young squire' who rose to become the 'Stalwart Knight' in *Idylls of the King* – while also sneering at the Chinese. *Had a superior being from a brighter sphere come down to assist us, the joy could not have been greater. His coat was pulled off, and there was a rush to the kitchen, where, the materials being all ready, the process was gone though, with an earnest and inquiringly crowd of pigtails around the table. The Chinese "boys" knew of the difficulty, and, from the way they watched the whole proceeding, I have no doubt that, with the Chinaman's powers of imitation, a perfect facsimile, even to the exact number of plums, will be produced by them on Christmas Day this year.*

The Soldiers' Church

On Christmas Day 1880 the *ILN* featured an illustration based upon a sketch drawn on site of officers and men from two infantry regiments and a battery of Royal Artillery attending a service conducted by a regimental chaplain. The commentary said *The red uniforms of the former, and blue of the latter, seated on rising banks of earth under the shade of tall pine-trees, had a rather good effect. The pulpit was a circular mound of earth raised at the foot of an opposite tree, and a drum served for the altar.* The service had taken place at the Peiwar Kotul, a mountainous pass in the Kuram Valley in Afghanistan, during the Second Anglo-Afghan War of 1878-80. It was an emotive spot for the British public. Here on 2 December 1878 Major General Frederick Roberts had become a national hero when British and Indian regiments under his command made a surprise night attack to defeat Afghan forces defending the Kuram Valley approach to the capital, Kabul.

The aggressive British military presence in Afghanistan was primarily to counter Russian influence building up and threatening India. Early in 1879 a new Emir of Afghanistan ceded control of his country's foreign affairs to Great Britain whose forces now occupied much of the country. However an uprising in Kabul led to further battles, and it took until September 1880 for General Roberts to finally crush the Afghans at the battle of Kandahar. Robert's determined, and sometimes desperate, 320 mile march from Kabul to lift the Afghan's siege of Kandahar quickly entered into Imperial legend and the repertoires of popular music hall performers.

The *ILN*'s Christmas Day picture that year was therefore seen as an entirely appropriate celebration of a hard-fought victory earlier in the war that had caught the public imagination. Few perhaps recalled that Indian regiments formed the greater part of Robert's forces. In later years after other successes the national hero became Field Marshal Earl Roberts of Kandahar (1832-1914).

The Soldiers' Church
– ILN 25 December 1880.

Christmas Day entertainment to the troops at Port Said – ILN 13 January 1883

Christmas Day Entertainment to the Troops at Port Said

Early in January 1883 the *ILN* featured *Christmas Day Entertainment to the Troops at Port Said*. It was based upon a sketch by a Royal Marine officer who attended the event which the town's inhabitants, or at least the ones with influence and money, had organised and paid for. The garrison comprised two companies of Royal Marines and one of Royal Artillery. Its barracks, until recently a store shed, *was handsomely decorated with flags, coloured paper, and such few evergreens as could be got at Port Said; the candelabra were of a remarkably novel design. The band of the Egyptian gunboat Sakir, by permission of her commanding officer, played during the repast.... All the Egyptian officials of Port Said were present, the British officers, and the leading inhabitants, representing many nationalities.* After the dinner *the men rose and chaired their officers, carrying them round the table with hearty cheers, which rather astonished the natives.*

Port Said was created in 1859 at the start of the construction of the Suez Canal by the French engineer Ferdinand de Lesseps. Between then and the canal opening in 1869 Port Said's population reached 10,000, and kept on growing as an important trading centre where two continents met and a key place in the operation of the canal at its entrance from the Mediterranean Sea. The 120 mile canal cut 5,500 miles off the sea route between the Arabian Sea and London, and an acute awareness of its strategic as well as commercial significance led the British to pay the bankrupt Khedive Isma'il Pasha of Egypt £4,000,000 in 1875 for his 44% holding. In 1882 the British crushed an Egyptian army revolt against Khedive Tewfik Pasha, largely fuelled by unrest at foreign interference in Egyptian affairs. They stayed on as occupiers and protectors of the Khedive, the canal and British and foreign investments until well into the twentieth century. After this popular victory the *ILN*'s image of the 1882 Christmas dinner in Port Said was a satisfying seasonal sign of everything going Great Britain's way.

Turkey in Egypt: Christmas in Cairo

A few years later, in the 1886 Christmas Supplement, a striking picture by George Lucas Seymour showed an Arab boy in Cairo delivering a Christmas turkey. The accompanying verse arrogantly exclaimed:

He's bound for the barracks, this sutler so sable –
This myrmidon dark of the indolent east;
And Turkey shall furnish a good Christian table
While England in Egypt presides at the feast.

The Turkish Sultan still retained notional authority over Egypt's Khedive but, as *ILN* readers appreciated that Christmas, it was Great Britain that had the greatest say over the country's affairs.

George Lucas Seymour: Turkey in Egypt: Christmas in Cairo – ILN 1886 Christmas Supplement.

Sending Home Christmas Greetings from the River Nile

On 13 December 1884 an apparently peaceful scene of men on a River Nile steamboat sending home Christmas greetings belied the grim reality of what was happening. The boat was approaching Wadi Halfa on the Egyptian border with the Sudan, where in October 1884 an army led by General Sir Garnet Wolseley arrived by steamers towing numerous whalers to relieve Khartoum, hundreds of miles to the south. Here Major General Charles Gordon was besieged by forces of the Mahdi, the self-styled leader of the Muslim Sudanese forces determined to rid the country of all invaders, be they Egyptian or British. Great Britain had been wracked by controversy over whether or not its interest in Egypt should extend to the Sudan, and when Gordon was besieged another controversy erupted over whether he could resist the Mahdi or needed to be rescued. In the end a rescue mission was ordered, and reports of its progress coupled with messages smuggled out of an increasingly desperate Khartoum kept the nation on a knife-edge of excitement.

During December 1884 and through Christmas and the New Year Wolseley's hard-pressed forces advanced past the Nile's dangerous cataracts, and realising time was running out a force riding camels was sent across the desert to Khartoum only to arrive on 28 January 1885 two days after the city fell. General Gordon had been killed. *ILN* readers looking at this illustration might well have looked with pride at British enterprise and courage – if also thinking (as many did) that the Sudan was not worth occupying – but there was widespread trust that General Gordon, who was fast becoming a national hero, would be rescued. Instead he was soon to be revered as a martyr, and Prime Minister Gladstone's dithering over ordering the relief expedition would lose him the 1885 election.

Christmas Day on Board a Training Ship

Eager boys crowding around a large plum pudding adorned with royal and naval ensigns greeted readers of the *ILN* on Christmas Eve 1887. Plates were being grabbed, spoons waved, a mug has been spilled and there is a sense that the celebration will soon become boisterous. It is Christmas Day on board a naval training ship, and many of the boys had had a less than happy start in life. The *ILN* delicately explained the situation. The ships were *among the various industrial training institutions for English boys of the class needing public assistance to provide for their education and to fit them for manly service to their country. It is pleasant at Christmas to know that they enjoy, like most boys in. happy homes, their due share of the festive treats and harmless fun of the season.*

In the Thames, Mersey and Clyde and ports such as Plymouth and Portsmouth more than two dozen capacious old ships with fixed off-shore moorings became home and school for boys gleaned from orphanages, workhouses and other impoverished families. *These vessels are placed under the care of experienced officers and trustworthy instructors who combine the discipline of the ship with that of a school; and the boys, more easily kept together and subjected to common rules than in most boarding schools on shore, acquire an esprit de corps, and a habit of cheerful and willing obedience, which are the most essential conditions*

Sending home Christmas messages from the River Nile – ILN 13 December 1884.

of preparing them for the duties of active life. Those deemed suitable went into the Royal Navy or Mercantile Marine. In 1870 the *ILN* had featured the unappealing hulk of an old timber warship much like those used as training ships.

Early training ships were attached to the charitable Marine Society, largely to remove boys from the malign influence of workhouses and slums, and from 1855 the Royal Navy established its own training ships. Boys entered them around the age of 11 and stayed until 15 or 16; discipline was strict, the birch was ever-present, and food usually limited to meat, biscuit and potatoes. There were the usual basic elementary school lessons plus the basic skills of seamanship. Although the regime was demanding, and indeed harsh, the general public, the Poor Law authorities, parents and, possibly, the boys themselves recognised its worth in terms of training, careers, self-esteem, and superiority to the demeaning and demoralising life of a pauper.

Richard Taylor: Christmas Day on board a training ship – ILN 24 December 1887.

Samuel Phillips Jackson: The Royal Navy: The Past – ILN 24 December 1870.

The Signalman's Christmas Dinner

The Signalman's Christmas Dinner by the Anglo French artist Amedee Forestier (1854-1930) appeared on 27 December 1890. *The signalman, who has not been able to get his Christmas holiday this year, was at his post for the first morning train at 5.25 a.m. and will be at it, we understand, until the 11.8 p.m. night down express from London has rushed without stopping past this lonely station.... He must be ever on the watch.* The long hours, and their threat to staff health and public safety, were a regular complaint by railwaymen's unions. *Our hearty sympathy attends his solitary repast, which is furnished, let us hope, with two or three extra luxuries, but which he must consume amid the chill snows of December... Is it the kind-hearted old station-master, with his own meal, who has stepped out to eat in company, cheering this good fellow by some words of friendly talk?*

The picture and commentary convey much about the late Victorian railway system in operation, and notably the great responsibility held by a lowly member of the company's staff. Here, the commentary says, he has pulled the lever on the nearby signal to allow the express freight (as indicated by the two lamps on the locomotive's smoke box) through his section of track, and then returned to his warm fire to watch the train pass by. The rolled up flags for use in emergency lie by the side of the hut. Unusually for 1890, it seems this stretch of line remained without a mechanical signal box. After their invention by John Saxby in the mid 1850s, they had spread slowly across much, but clearly not all, of the growing network between the 1860s and 1880s.

Amedee Forestier: The Signalman's Christmas Dinner – ILN 27 December 1890.

New Year's greetings by telephone – ILN 7 January 1882.

New Year's Greetings by Telephone

On 7 January 1882 a picture entitled *New Year's Greetings by Telephone* showed men and women in evening attire taking time out to enjoy the exciting new invention. The *ILN* enthused that *The wonderful performances of applied physical science at the present day have gone far towards annihilating both space and time, as natural obstacles to human correspondence and intercourse of thought.* The commentary gave few details beyond saying the scene was one of several in recent days in London where people could *satisfy themselves of the powers of the telephone, were enabled to use the miraculous hearing tubes, applied to their own ears, and could listen to words spoken in another place by the aid of the conducting wires.* However the *ILN* was quick to point out that if the range was ever significantly extended *The clock does not strike twelve simultaneously all round the world, nor has the sun been ordained to perform the impossible task of shining, at noon, upon all places at once.*

Throughout the nineteenth century several inventors had raced to transmit sounds using electrical power, including the Italian-American Antonio Meucci and German Johann Reis but identifiable speech proved elusive, until two Americans, Elisha Grey and Alexander Graham Bell, working independently on transmitters and receivers filed for patents on the same day, 14 February 1876. As Bell's was a few hours earlier, his was awarded. Refinements were quick to follow. Bell's variable-resistance transmitter quickly improved the range to several miles, and Thomas Edison's carbon microphone soon dominated receivers. In 1878 the first machines with the transmitter and receiver in the same handle were manufactured, and in 1879 the first small London telephone exchange opened. The first international call (between New Brunswick in Canada and Maine in the USA) was made on 1 July 1881.

Frederick George Cotman: An Anxious Heart – ILN *1876 Christmas Supplement.*

Horace Petherick: Steering for Home – ILN *1876 Christmas Supplement.*

The Sea

Paintings of ships at sea were popular, not least because seaside holidays were popular, and pride rode high regarding the nation's naval and mercantile supremacy. Equally popular were paintings of vulnerable women, especially young ones, as expressions of the fragility of their lives in the face of disasters, especially the death of fathers or husbands upon whose earnings and protection they were entirely dependent. And as every reader of the *ILN* knew, numerous ships were lost at sea, and the British coastline was littered with wrecks.

The 1876 Christmas Supplement was thought particularly appropriate to show two emotionally charged images. The picture of the desperate sailors wrestling with the storm was by Horace Petherick (1839-1919); the anxious young wife standing barefoot in squally weather on the cliff top was by Frederick George Cotman (1850-1920). Put together, the pair created a particularly dramatic story for comfortable fireside readers at Christmas – and the ending, whether happy or sad, remains shrouded in mystery.

CHAPTER SEVEN

Christmas Games and Pastimes: Enjoyment with an Edge

A Visit to the Old Folk on Christmas Eve

A Visit to the Old Folk on Christmas Eve by Alfred Hunt (1830-96) appeared on Christmas Eve 1864, and reinforced the comforting Victorian conviction that a well-balanced mutually supporting family life was the source of all happiness. It took for granted that the husband's role was essentially that of bread-winner, treasurer and major decision maker and the wife provided the softer virtues of home maker, child rearer, nurse and moral guide. The wife might appear to be the junior partner but she was often eulogised

Alfred Hunt: A Visit to the Old Folk on Christmas Eve – ILN 24 December 1864.

as the vital guardian of the family's domestic comfort, integrity and standing. The family Christmas became the much sought after Victorian ideal, and owed much to the many poets, artists, novelists and commentators who kept telling the world how morally and physically corrosive industrialisation had become as it spread across the land with its smoke polluted cities, dehumanising mass production processes, harsh competitiveness, and absence of moral and religious constraints.

The commentary epitomised the trend. *Home is the parent and protector of all the virtues. Round the domestic hearth they most thoroughly ripen, as in their native soil and clime. Watching the great maelstrom of business in our cities, and thinking of the hardening tendency of money getting pursuits, and the wear and tear of life, mental as well as physical, one is thankful to know that most of the persons thus fiercely engaged in the battle of life have homes, where, at the close of each day's work, they repose in slippered ease, surrounded by the softening and purifying influence of the household deities....Nor is it among the wealthy alone that home exercises its beneficial influence. The poorest, except for a few unhappy outcasts, bask also in its sacred warmth.*

Here we have (in the illustration on page 97) *one of the well-to-do families – not rich and certainly not poor – with which England abounds.... The first hearty greeting over, the young mother, with natural pride, shows her baby to its grandmother.... A boy and girl rush gleesomely to their grandfather; and soon, you may be sure, they will be perched on his knee, rifling his pockets.... Tenderly the father is about to lift from the holly covered cart their youngest, except the baby in arms...The eldest daughter – father's pride and mother's delight – like a good daughter and an attentive sister, has stayed in the cart to assist the others safely out. One sees at a glance that she is mother's right hand: she quickly lulls baby to sleep, settles disputes between the younger ones in a twinkling, has needle and thread always at hand to fasten a loose button or repair a rent, does not disdain to darn stockings, is a notable maker of pies and puddings, and is, in short, skilled in all household lore....Yet she is a true daughter of Eve. See! the sly creature holds a branch of mistletoe in her hand, too precious a treasure to be trusted to other's care.... One would not be greatly surprised if the youth by the door, too timid, seemingly, to offer his assistance to the fair girl on whom his gaze is so ardently fastened, were to take heart of grace, and, waxing bolder by acquaintance, claim, and, after a struggle more or less hard, gain from her a kiss under its milky-white berries.*

The Family Christmas

On Christmas Day 1847 the *ILN* devoted several pages to what it considered a typical well-to-do family's festivities. A key illustration showed the extended family comfortably gathered together in a grand room complete with gaslights and holly decorated family portraits. It represented the Victorian ideal of a cross generational family providing its members with a refuge from the outside world and also a springboard for its younger members to make a success of their lives through careers and marriage. Men generated an income in the outside world, and women created a caring and well-ordered world within the home. Domestic stability contributed much to the stability of society as a whole, and provided a role model for children. Christmas was its celebration *par excellence*, with generous hearts healing any jealousies and dislikes. In the illustration the servants were absent, no doubt clearing away the last meal and preparing the next one, and any employees have been left to their own devices (unlike the old-fashioned Fezziwigs in *The Christmas Carol*).

The commentary claimed that *custom immemorial hath stamped the Family Party at Christmas as the most sincere and genuine meeting of the whole year. Many an imagined wrong, and many a heartburn is soothed by the season of hallowed mirth. The sweet sanctity of its association seems to shut out all meaner joys. Well, the party have left the substantial luxuries of the dinner table, and are now enjoying the more refined delights that spring from the interchange of affection reared around the same hearth – the same fond home.*

View the deepening circle: the grandfather, in his easy Ashburnham chair, his heart brimming over with gladness. Opposite are seated the matrons of the party, whose delight in "talking over old times", is one of those touches of nature that the painter loves – his conversation scenes. To be brief, in this beaming circle we see almost every phase of existence – from the cradle to the grave; old age watching the gambols of early childhood; in short, mid-age, manhood, and youth.

Home for the Holidays

On 23 December 1848 *Home for the Holidays* by Harrison Weir (1824-1906) featured a mode of travel fast becoming redundant as railways spread across the land. It is getting dark, and the

The family Christmas – ILN 25 December 1847.

coach, perhaps specially commissioned for the occasion, with its four steaming horses has finally arrived at the lodge gate of a country house to deposit a young man home from boarding school for Christmas. Some of his school fellows are waving him off before they carry on their journey. He is greeted by his mother and younger brother and sister while uniformed footmen take hold of his luggage. Other friends or relatives on ponies are there to meet the coach.

The *ILN* asked: *Who does not recollect the joyousness of Breaking-up – the uproarious mirth of Going Home – and the affectionate Welcome on reaching there? There is nothing in after-life to efface the recollection of these happy hours..... At last "Going Home Day"*

arrives. The night has been one of restless anticipation. The boys, who will have a long journey, in all probability rise before daylight. The breakfast is soon despatched. The well-appointed coach reaches the door, and is soon freighted with its joyous lads. And then commences the fun of the road, with peashooters and volleys of peas fired at wonder-struck gazers; the horn twanging through the silent villages: and a host of practical jokes, such as boys alone can play....The boys feel, as it were, "let loose"; their ecstasy knows no bounds; they whoop and halloo most lustily.

The illustration and commentary no doubt reminded many middle-class readers of their own early nineteenth century boarding schools, and the endurance (as many accounts tell) of much rote-learning of Classical literature, harsh punishments, poor food, and routine bullying, as well as, perhaps, the forging of useful friendships. The commentary sympathised with the boys' fervent wish to go home at Christmas, and saw the assaults by the privileged offspring of the well-to-do on the people they pass as entirely excusable pranks.

Over three decades later, on Christmas Eve 1881, *A Christmas journey as we used to do it* by Alfred Emslie (1848-1918) more than hinted at the acute discomfort of such journeys in cramped and unwieldy vehicles across often ill-kept roads. Nevertheless an accompanying poem by Mason Jackson recalled the excitement of roughing it on the outside seats as the wind, rain and sleet stung faces and froze fingers. No doubt it reflected the nostalgia for wintery stage-coach scenes already pervading Victorian Christmas cards. In practice, the trains had long won the day in relatively smooth riding, protection from the elements, shorter journey time, and expected time of arrival. However horse drawn vehicles had several decades of life left in them, primarily as links to stations from areas the railways had not yet reached.

Alfred Edward Emslie: A Christmas Journey as we used to do it – ILN 24 December 1881.

Harrison Weir: Home for the Holidays – ILN 23 December 1848.

The Arrival of the Christmas Train

On 21 December 1850 an illustration highlighted the dramatic changes in transport taking place that were both enabling and encouraging families to get-together at Christmas. The *Arrival of the Christmas Train* by Edward Duncan (1803-82) pictures the hectic scene at Bishopsgate Station, then the London Terminus of the Eastern Counties Railway, as passengers emerge and porters handle the vast array of luggage stored on the outside roof racks and in the special goods van at the rear of the train – but nearest the viewer. The locomotives are in the distance.

The poem spots the goods chaotically lying around.

Has the Parcels Train arrived?
– Have you Michaelmas survived?
See you not it has? What else
The traffic and strife compels?
What brings those oysters row on row,
That marvellous pile, that wondrous show,
Those countless scores of ducks and geese,
Those pheasants, turkeys – prophecies
Of coming hospitalities?
That Train, like a chest, so titanic in size,
Is a shrine that holds gifts for both simple and wise.

Bishopsgate was a two level station opened in 1840 at the junction of Shoreditch High Street and Bethnal Green Road. Between 1875 and 1879 it gradually closed to passenger traffic, being replaced by the larger Liverpool Street terminus, and was rebuilt as a goods station.

Edward Duncan: The Arrival of the Christmas Train – ILN 21 December 1850.

Gabriel Nicolet: Snap–Dragon – ILN *28 December 1889.*

Snap-Dragon

The *ILN*'s Christmas editions for 1847 and 1889 featured groups of children playing the popular game of snap-dragon. Raisins and sometimes almonds are thrown into a large dish of brandy which is then set alight, and the children pluck the fruit and nuts out of the blazing brandy and eat them – hopefully without burning their hands or scalding their lips. The *ILN* said an eerie ghost-like effect from the smoke and blue tongues of fire added atmosphere to the event. *The sport affords much fun in a darkened room; not the least of which is the spectral appearance of the young players from the spirit flame.* In the illustration in 1889 by the French artist Gabriel Nicolet (1856-1921) it looked as though a young boy had been burned.

Sometimes a song was chanted. One recorded in Robert Chambers' *Book of Days,* published in 1864, went:

Here he comes with flaming bowl,
Don't he mean to take his toll,
Snip! Snap! Dragon!

Take care you don't take too much,
Be not greedy in your clutch,
Snip! Snap! Dragon!

With his blue and lapping tongue
Many of you will be stung
Snip! Snap! Dragon!

For her snaps at all that comes
Snatching at his feast of plums
Snip! Snap! Dragon!

A Magic Lantern Show

On Christmas Day 1858 the *ILN* featured Henry Hine's (1811-95) picture of children at a Christmas party watching a magic lantern show. In a darkened room a light provided by candles as here, and later by an electric lamp, shone through an image on glass to project it on a larger scale on a wall (although white walls in Victorian middle class homes were a great rarity) or, as here, a white sheet. Here everyone is enjoying a humorous image of an English sailor stopping a hapless Chinese officer in his tracks. The image referred to the recent British victories in the Second Opium War against China. The Qing rulers of China sought to stop British merchants selling Indian grown opium in China, but both wars (1839-42) and (1856-1860) saw British arms, and especially its naval power, defeat Chinese forces. After the British fleet had captured the Pearl River forts and bombarded Canton the Treaty of Tientsin in June 1858 forced the reluctant Chinese to grant extensive trading rights to the West. Further fighting into 1860 led to the British occupation of Beijing and the Imperial Forbidden City palace.

The *ILN* said slides included *a jolly Jack Tar taking a tender farewell of his sweetheart previous to embarking for the "Eastern Hingees and parts beyond the seas", in H.M.S. Tremendous, which we see floating gallantly over the deep blue waves in the distance. This touching opening of the pictorial epic is followed by a poetical view of the Isle of Wight by moonlight – the Needles are* *visible bearing N.N.W. by compass and the Tremendous, with her studding sails and spanker-booms all set, appears gradually melting away.* At this moment, to everyone's surprise and joy, a hidden musical-box plays 'Then farewell my trim built wherry'.

In the succeeding tableau a storm rages, the good ship is soon tossed on the mountain billows, lightnings flash, and dismal thunder (elicited by a confederate from a teatray) makes the hearts of the sympathising children shudder; thick clouds overspread the scene, and the spectators are left in doubt and darkness, while the musical-box interprets "The Bay of Biscay" in truly artistic style. What has become of poor Jack? ..... Is he gone down in his ship? Not a bit of it. Hooray! There he is! He has escaped and landed in the Flowery Land where the British Lion is making small change of the Celestials. Our friend Jack, anxious to possess a real live Chinaman, has made fast to Commissioner Yeh's pigtail, by which he means to tow him alongside, to the appropriate music of "Yo, heave ho!" Again the scene is changed, and the nautical drams concludes with the Sailor's Hornpipe, danced at Portsmouth by Jack and his sweetheart, amid the tumultuous applause and acclamations of the spectators.

Ye Mingchen was a senior Chinese official and bitter opponent of British influence, especially during the Opium Wars, but was unable to resist British naval and military might. He was captured and imprisoned by the British in 1858, and frequently derided in newspapers and journals – and, it seems, slide shows.

Henry George Hine: The Magic Lantern Show – ILN *25 December 1858.*

The Shadow Dance

In the 1861 Christmas Supplement *The Shadow Dance* by Hablot Knight Browne (1815-82) featured another practical approach to story telling *where by a simple arrangement on the illuminated calico the shadow of the card figure can be cast and made to perform all manner of terpsichorean eccentricities. Here you may see Punch and Judy, modified in shape and Italianised into elegance, dance the most fantastic of dances, both curiously and furiously – dance, in a word, "like mad" – tossing about arms and legs in fashion preternatural, for surely no man or woman of real flesh and blood ever made so queer a use of either. And yet they are but shadows of pasteboard, impaled on wires, and moved briskly about by the hand of mortal.* Initially the *ILN* thought the 'shadow dance' should incorporate moral lessons for the young audience, but on reflection said that homely and amusing entertainment was perfectly acceptable at Christmas.

Hablot Knight Browne: The Shadow Dance – ILN 1861 Christmas Supplement.

A Model Theatre & Little Red Riding Hood

The 1861 Christmas Supplement devoted a detailed page on how to make and work a model theatre to entertain parents, friends and relatives. The stage was a simple frame of wood with a solid bottom to stand on a table and with several moveable bars of wood lying across the top. Scenery for the various acts in a play was painted on boards, and hung from the bars of wood as required. The characters are made from wooden cones which *can be brought from a turner for about one shilling a dozen*. They are dressed from odd bits of material and faces drawn on the round top, and stand on a pin fixed to a flat piece of wood that enables the character to move about on stage without seeming to be controlled.

The instructions came complete with a surprisingly sophisticated play based on the story of Little Red Riding Hood, a favourite Victorian pantomime. The backgrounds were a fairy landscape, Red Riding Hood's cottage, the forest, and Grandmother's cottage. The characters were Mother Bunch (the fairy narrator), Patty Dumple (Red Riding Hood), Dame Dumple (her mother), and the Wolf. There was a lot for the children providing the voices to learn – by rote the *ILN* suggested – and no shortage of mounting threat in the story. For example, as Red Riding Hood sets out to visit her grandmother with a basket of newly baked bread and a pot of butter her mother warns:

*Three miles your journey, and it's half past two
so, mind, don't loiter on the way*

Red Riding Hood. *Not I
I'll walk as fast as almost as bird can fly.
And though I love to hear the throstle sing,
And watch the rabbits o'er the greensward spring,
Or sit upright, and with his furry toes
Smooth his long ears and rub his sooty nose,
And love to gather, as I onward pass,
Wood-sorrel, foxgloves, and the long spear grass.
I'll not be tempted, though, perhaps, you'll say
Already I have loitered on my way.
One kiss, dear mother. I shall not be late.*

The scene changes to the forest. Enter the wolf.
*I don't know what's the cause, but I am ailing:
I'm nervous, and my appetite is failing,
At breakfast I could eat but one poor kid;
At lunch two little lambs were all I did:
And what to have for dinner? – that's the question;
It must be something easy of digestion.
There's an old goose I know of, but she's tough;
Besides, one goose would scarcely be enough.
Ah! What is this? (Sniffs) 'Tis something very sweet!
Little Red Riding Hood? There is a treat (Hides himself)*

A model theatre and Little Red Riding Hood – ILN *1861 Christmas Supplement.*

Kenny Meadows: Blindman's Bluff – ILN 1849 Christmas Supplement.

Blindman's Bluff & Forfeits

Cartoons by Kenny Meadows in the 1849 Christmas Supplement highlighted two more popular games. In Blindman's Buff a person is blindfolded, disoriented by being turned around and then required to capture and identify another person from the group who have scattered around the room out of his/her way. The commentary to Meadows' picture notes that the hilarity amongst the men and children is caused by the elderly woman on the right about to lose her lace cap and peruke (a false front of hair) as well as her dignity, and the stout woman on the left being surprised by the hefty pull on her skirts. Apparently the child rolling on the floor is having a temper tantrum. Decorous is not the word to describe this Victorian scene.

The second picture by Kenny Meadows pictures a game of Forfeits underway. One player (called the judge) leaves the rom while each of the others places a small personal item onto a tray. The judge returns to the room, selects an object and describes it. The owner must identify him/herself and pay a forfeit to get it back. Usually a list of forfeits has been drawn beforehand but the judge chooses the forfeit to be paid by the owner, and usually this is something amusing, but possibly embarrassing, such as sing a song, do a solo dance, tell a story, rub your head and pat your stomach, hug the person opposite you, or hop around the room. *Or picture yourself*, said the commentary, *having to whistle some tune through the keyhole without once laughing....or to look fixedly at the candle for five minutes without once smiling.*

Kenny Meadows: Forfeits – ILN 1849 Christmas Supplement.

Pictorial Charades

Charades were very popular, and the pictorial sequence was just one version. More commonly charades involved acting out the parts of a word (such as 'high/way/man' or 'Bucking/ham/ Pal/ace') or the title of a book or play.

Other versions included acting out What Am I Doing? and Tableaux Vivants (Living Pictures) which involved people in the 'frozen' representation of a famous event. The action was not limited to mime, and complicated charades could involve action and speech. (Answers at bottom of page.)

Pictorial Charades – ILN *1883 Christmas Supplement.*

FIRST SYLLABLE. SECOND SYLLABLE. THIRD SYLLABLE. THE WORD.

NO. 2.

FIRST SYLLABLE. SECOND SYLLABLE. THIRD SYLLABLE. THE WORD.

NO. 3.

FIRST SYLLABLE. SECOND SYLLABLE. THIRD SYLLABLE. THE WORD.

NO. 4.

FIRST SYLLABLE. SECOND SYLLABLE. THIRD SYLLABLE. THE WORD.

Answers 1. Handicap. 2. Polygon. 3. Hydraulic. 4. Gondolier.

Christmas Parties

On Christmas Day 1886 two drawings were issued together. *A Christmas Party: Warm and Welcome* by E.J.Walker featured nine boys and girls from well-to-do families chatting on a staircase in their expensive party clothes. They know each other well, and seem to be arranged on the stairs in three groups – the oldest at the bottom, and the youngest at the top. *A Christmas Party: Out in the Cold* by Augustus Mulready (1844-1904), well known for his pictures of Victorian street life, features a group of thinner boys and girls of varying ages, all in plainer, patched and ragged clothing, eagerly climbing on and peering through the railings into a grand room where Christmas festivities are at their height. One boy is a street sweeper eking a living clearing a passage across the road through the horse dung and other rubbish for women with

E.J.Walker: A Christmas Party: Warm & Welcome – ILN *25 December 1886.*

Augustus Mulready: A Christmas Party: Out in the Cold – ILN 25 December 1886.

long clothes and men with highly polished shoes. The older girl has a goose in her basket, and the boy beside her has some mistletoe, which suggests they are a notch up the economic ladder from the abject poor. All of them have that most coveted of Victorian items of clothing – a sound pair of boots. The accompanying single verse poems see the activities in each illustration as the natural expressions of childhood. The rich are totally absorbed in their own enjoyment while the poor are happy enough to admire an out-of-reach lifestyle without being troubled by envy. If believed, it was a comforting pair of pictures for *ILN* readers on Christmas Day. They could also comfort themselves that by 1886 the vast majority

of working class children were attending school, at least for a few years, and thereby imbuing the government controlled curriculum heavy on the basic skills, Imperial history, patriotic literature, and Christian teaching.

The children of the rich, in gay new dresses
Stray on the stairs, from dancing at their ball;
Their house shines bright, with Fortune's fond caresses;
Childhood's bright spirit is a gift to all.

The children of the poor, with hearts as bright –
Save those who hunger, or are pinched with cold –
Peep in, rejoicing at the festive light;
For childhood knows not envy, and is bold.

Under the Mistletoe

The Greeks and Romans had used mistletoe as a medicine, and the first century Druids saw it as a symbol of fertility and new life as it often flowered in winter. These positive, yet pagan, associations lingered into the Christian era, and although it was not considered appropriate as a church decoration, mistletoe retained some of its legacy as a festive opportunity for securing a kiss with serious, or not so serious, intentions. Possibly it was an unusual example of a habit among the servants of a household spreading up the social hierarchy.

Under the Mistletoe by Lucien Davis appeared in the *ILN*'s 1891 Christmas Supplement. It shows a boy standing on a chair embracing and kissing his beautiful mother under a bough of mistletoe helpfully held over them by his sister. Rather languidly she is turning and looking lovingly at him, and although the wealthy family is dressed formally, perhaps for dinner or a reception, everyone seems relaxed. Nevertheless the children's actions involving the mistletoe and pole seem to have been the result of planning and hope, and not merely a momentary impulse.

The embrace and kiss resonate with the powerful Victorian assumption that the boy is of an age, and in a social strata, when maternal influences were expected to be replaced by immersion in the wholly male environment of a socially exclusive boarding school. The regimes in such potentially fearsome institutions were highly regarded as the entirely appropriate training ground for gentlemen of leisure, members of parliament, and those hopeful of high rank in the civil service, legal profession and Anglican Church. However, as many memoirs recall, the boys lives within the classroom were characterised by interminable rote learning and harsh punishments, and outside the classroom by bullying, poor food, periodic epidemics, and a heavy emphasis on strenuous sports. One wonders, too, how often the boy saw his mother, as wet nurses and nannies assumed many maternal duties from birth, and many wealthy parents usually enjoyed hectic social lives in town and country without their children. Perhaps this kiss was a rare opportunity to gain affection when the family gathered at Christmas, and perhaps he was already experiencing the challenges of boarding school life and was home merely for the brief holiday.

The illustration can be said to retain some of the innocence of the pre-Freudian age, as the publication of Sigmund Freud's controversial works describing and naming the Oedipus Complex was still a few years away. His *Interpretation of Dreams* dates from 1899 and *A Special Type of Choice of Object made by Men* from 1910. In Classical Greek mythology Oedipus unwittingly killed his father and married his mother, and Freud adopted the term in his argument that many boys sometimes consciously, sometimes unconsciously, sexually desire their mothers while hating their fathers.

Lucien Davis: Under the Mistletoe – ILN 1891 Christmas Supplement.

The Attack on the Redoubt

Several Christmas illustrations glorify war and military valour. *The Attack on the Redoubt* by Walter Jenks Morgan (1847-1924) appeared in the 1877 Christmas Supplement. It showed well-dressed children behaving less than decorously as they attacked and defended a redoubt made out of domestic furniture. The battle has occurred, the commentary asserts, because *the children have, in the last six months, overheard so much talk of military slaughter in the daily conversation of newspaper-reading elders, who ought to know better, that not only young Tom, Dick and Harry, but Ethel, Minnie and Kitty, are fired with the ambition of martial exploits.*

The story is that the owner of the house, a valiant Colonel with a Victoria Cross, has indulged Tom, his grandson, in his fondness for toy guns and soldiers and his aspirations of gaining a commission in the Royal Artillery. At their 1877 Christmas party, Tom, his sister Ethel, and their friends decided to play out the Siege of Plevna. This was a celebrated battle that had lasted from 20 July until 10 December that year in the war Russia and Romania were fighting to free part of the Balkans from the Ottoman Empire. Public opinion in Great Britain generally favoured the liberation campaign, but the heroic, if ultimately doomed, defence of the fortified town of Plevna by the heavily outnumbered Turkish forces led by Osman Pasha against repeated Russian and Romanian assaults captured the public imagination. The war had been widely reported, not least by the *ILN*'s correspondents on the spot.

Little Dick, with a red smoking jacket not unlike the Mussulman fez, stands for Osman Pasha. He mounts upon the armchair, while a breastwork, hastily made of other furniture, shelters the defending party. They ply their weapons to repulse the Grand Duke Nicholas, our young friend Tom, leading Ethel and General Skobeleff to the assault. The Grand Duke is knocked down with a sofa-cushion, but Plevna must be captured at any cost.

Grand Duke Nicholas Nikolaevich (1831-91) was a younger son of Tsar Nicholas I, and the nominal and inept Commander-in Chief of the Russian armies in the war.

General Mikhail Skobelev (1843-82) was one of Imperial Russia's ablest generals.

Osman Nuri Pasha (1832-1900) was the Turkish general who skilfully held back the larger Russian and Romanian armies from advancing into the Balkans.

Walter Jenks Morgan: The Attack on the Redoubt – ILN 1877 Christmas Supplement.

Richard Caton Woodville: A Seasonal Compliment – ILN 1 January 1881.

A Seasonal Compliment: Crowning the Hero

On new Year's Day 1881 *A Seasonal Compliment: Crowning the Hero* by Richard Caton Woodville (1856-1927), a prolific painter of military scenes and battles, featured a group of adoring young women adorning an army officer with an evergreen wreath and coronet as he arrived at a Christmas party on his return from the recent campaign in Afghanistan. The hard fought Second Afghan War of 1878-1880 had ended that September with the decisive defeat of Amir Ayub Khan by General Roberts at Kandahar and his replacement by Abdur Rahman Khan who was more amenable to British demands.

Tongue in cheek the *ILN* asserted that young women thought all officers were naturally brave and *entitled, man for man, to a larger share of feminine regard than their brothers in the civil professions.* Equally facetiously it asserted *that few sensible men, who do not happen to wear the Queen's uniform, will entertain the slightest jealousy of those social attentions which are commonly bestowed on those who do.* And unlike French or Prussian officers *and their frequent assumption of personal superiority to other classes of their fellow-countrymen, we seldom or never meet with an Englishman of any commissioned rank in the Army, whose behaviour shows any disposition to claim an undue degree of importance in society on this account.*

Visiting The Tower of London in the Holidays

On 30 December 1871 an illustration showed a young girl dressed in the height of juvenile fashion being encouraged by her mother and father to listen to the stories told by a Yeoman Warder during their Christmas holiday tour of the Tower of London. The *ILN* harped upon the gloomy associations of the Traitors' Gate and the Bloody Tower, the executions of the Duke of Clarence in 1478 and Lady Jane Grey in 1554, and the murders of the young Edward V and his brother in 1483. It noted all the vicious weaponry on display, and then turned to the illustration: *But, ah! what have we here? Ancient instruments of torture and punishment – an iron collar of torture taken from the Spaniards in 1588, the "cravat", thumb-screws, and other dainty devices, by which* *contumacious prisoners were made pliable, and truth or falsehood (most frequently the latter) was rung from their racked victims. Our major-domo ... shows the use, up to a certain point, of the thumb-screw to a fair girl of the party – papa the while improving the occasion, and telling Miss Rosebud how thankful she ought to be that she was not born in the dark ages when she might have been racked, and (who knows) perhaps burnt at the stake for truth's sake. The young lady does not seem alive to the privilege of living in the nineteenth century, and looks upon the thumb-screw as a toy, though victims as graceful and innocent as she have writhed and groaned and fallen into a dead faint under its use.* It was a classic case of Victorian outings being earnestly educative if not necessarily wholly enjoyable, and the *ILN* being deliberately salacious under the guise of celebrating the advance of British political and religious attitudes.

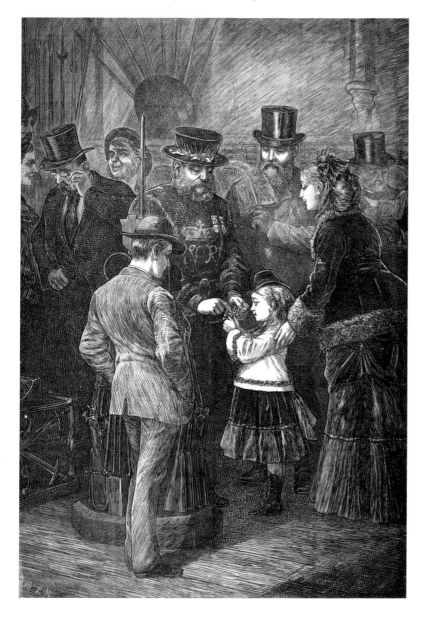

Visiting the Tower of London in the holidays – ILN 30 December 1871.

A Day's Ferreting in the Christmas Holidays – ILN 5 January 1867.

A Day's Ferreting in the Christmas Holidays

On 5 January 1867 the *ILN* celebrated an ancient winter sport with *A Day's Ferreting in the Christmas Holidays*. It shows several young lads from well-to-do rural families enjoying themselves with a gamekeeper and his young assistants as their ferrets are used to chase rabbits out of burrows into nets covering the entrances. Treated as troublesome vermin, they are then killed and bagged. *The Christmas holidays are the time for this pursuit, which may be followed with advantage in snowy weather, as the rabbits will then be at home. The scene represented in our illustration shows one of the most interesting moments of the ferreter's occupation. The old gamekeeper, who accompanies these boys and has the chief management of the whole affair, is just taking a rabbit from the net, whilst another rabbit has*

escaped, and is running away, in spite of the boy who has thrown himself frantically upon it, and sprawls in the snow, to the great amusement if his colleagues. A ferret is shown, as are the terrier and spaniel eager to chase and kill the rabbits who escape the net.

The *ILN* said participating in *the good sport of sending a ferret through a rabbit hole gives the boys as keen a pleasure as was ever enjoyed by the Old Shekarry, or his predecessor Nimrod, in "Hunting Grounds of the Old World".* It was an impressive claim. 'Old Shekarry' was the pseudonym of Major Henry Astbury Leveson (1828-75), a renowned big-game hunter and author of the book published a few years earlier celebrating his numerous kills around the world. Nimrod was the *nom de plume* of the soldier turned fox hunter Charles Apperley (1777-1843), a celebrated writer for *The Sporting Magazine*.

A Village Entertainment

On 20 December 1884 a chain of comic drawings by Joseph Priestly Atkinson (1841-1923) portrayed a seasonal village entertainment. The gently mocking account, ostensibly by a member of the audience, said it took place in the school-room where some of the banners and wreaths *had* *previously done duty at a recent Conservative demonstration, and, patriotically if somewhat inappropriately, called upon us to "Stand by our Peers".* *ILN* readers would have known this referred to the House of Lords opposition, strongly supported by many Conservatives, to the Liberal government's new Reform Bill extending the vote to many more members of the working classes.

Joseph Priestly Atkinson: A Village Entertainment – ILN 20 December 1884.

The rector welcomed everyone in his most paternal style and received *warm applause from the closely packed audience, who (such is the force of habit) had at the beginning settled themselves in their places with the half-sleepy and wholly dutiful air of expectancy which characterised them as a congregation on Sunday at sermon time.* The programme began with a classical piece by Mr Taffy, the general shopkeeper, on the violin, the schoolmaster on the flute and the rector' wife on the piano. Although the flute uttered startling wheezes and shrieks and the pianist's page turner brought the music to a complete standstill by upsetting the score book, the delighted audience cried for an encore.

At this point the squire and his family arrived. *The squire who had just dined struggled gallantly with a yawn all evening,* but the ladies enthusiastically clapped everyone. Young Wursel sang his own composition about a bold young man and his adventures courting Mary Ann which *was warmly appreciated by the farmers and their wives, who laughed till the tears rolled down their rosy cheeks. There were fifteen verses, and every verse ended with an interminable "Fol-de-rol" which was taken up with tremendous gusto by the audience.* Mr Dionysius Cope, the normally retiring young curate, surprised and delighted everyone with his spirited high falsetto readings from 'Mrs Caudle's Curtain Lectures'. Written by Douglas Jerrold (1803-57) these were an amusing series of nagging admonishments of a husband by his wife for his alleged misdemeanours.

A quartet sang several songs, not too distracted by the well-known hostility between the supporters of the rival sopranos, Miss Cutts *(a chit of a thing with no more voice than a mouse)* and Mrs Jowler *(her voice resembles the shriek of a locomotive).* The blacksmith's deep bass rendering of 'The Charge of the Light Brigade' *was electrifying. To hear him describe how 'Cannons to the right of um; cannons to the left of um; cannons in front of um; vollered and thoondered" made one's hair stand on end, and it was a positive relief when he retired, mopping the perspiration off his manly brow. Miss Bellairs is the acknowledged beauty of our village, and is engaged to be married to Mr Flamingo. They sang "The Naggletons" in a way which might seem to bode portentously for their future relations as man and wife; but which evoked appreciative cheers from Farmer Wursal, who is supposed to be rather under the plump thumb of his buxom "missus", so that when his loud "Bravo" was heard, everyone looked at him and*

laughed immoderately. The 'Naggletons' was a series of humorous sketches following the lives of an ill-matched couple published in *Punch* between 1862 and 1865.

The account ended with the news that charity towards those not invited to the event was the aim. *And so the performance came to a timely end. The poor of the parish got a good five pounds towards their Christmas cheer; and we all went home to supper, highly pleased with our evening.*

The Christmas Story in the Children's Hospital

Featured in the 1881 Christmas Supplement, *The Christmas Story in the Children's Hospital* drawn by Henry Robert Robertson (1839-1921) featured a frightening time in a young child's life while also hailing the progress in Victorian medical care. The scene is set in the new purpose-built Hospital for Sick Children at Great Ormond Street that was built between 1871 and 1875 in the gardens of the original 1850s hospital. Funded entirely by donations and subscriptions, it was one of the most fashionable charities in the country, being supported by the rich and famous, including Charles Dickens, Baroness Burdett-Couts (1814-1906: the richest women in Britain), other members of the aristocracy, senior clergy and the Royal Family. In 1880 it treated 1,047 in-patients and 14,522 out-patients. By this date nurses had in-house training and wore uniforms, and hygiene and good food were recognised as key components of recovery and disease control. The accompanying poem highlights several key Victorian themes – the virtue of charitable giving, the particular care women imbued with the Christian faith offer as nurses, the Christian attitude towards death, and the comfort the Christmas story can bring.

*Nor praise, nor thanks, they ask, who here
The Children's Hospital attend
But spare its funds a half per cent
Of gold that you may save or spend*

*Then, if at Christmas you may taste
A pleasure, worldly minds know not,
Visit the Children's Hospital,
And muse besides an infants's cot*

Here see the Christian woman's hand
Bring comfort to the wasting frame,
While from her faithful lips is heard
Our common Father's holy name

Around this Nurse, this patient, crowd
Some other children, growing well;
This child may die or live – who knows?
Of her – or us – we cannot tell

This only have we'd learnt: of all,
The never-dying soul is Love;
On Christmas Day the Child was born,
Who lived and died this truth to prove.

THE CHRISTMAS STORY she repeats,
To cheer the weary, painful hours,
Has comforted all human griefs,
And may relieve the worst of hours.

Henry Robert Robertson: The Christmas Story in the Children's Hospital – ILN
1881 Christmas Supplement.

The Cosy Old Maids & Crusty Old Bachelors

The 1889 Christmas Supplement included two striking drawings by Frederick Barnard (1846-96) who was celebrated for his illustrations in the novels of Charles Dickens published in the decade after the author's death in 1870. In the *Cosy Old Maids' Christmas* the decorated fireplace and glowing fire, the maid and tea tray, cat and kittens, pair of dogs, pampered monkey, parrot on the back of the chair, glass domed fruit display, comfortable furniture, and well made clothes and adornments highlight the satisfying if modest comfort in which these ladies live without the presence of men. The accompanying poem adds:

Blest are the souls which, having lost, or never having known,
The sweets of dear domestic life, disdain to mope and moan;
But gladly give a helping hand where'er they find distress,
Or live, as shown above, a life of Single Blessedness

Behold with what an air Miss B, with pets on every side,
Joined by her spinster friend, Miss C, welcomes blithe Christmastide.
But, bless me! on the chimney piece, are kissing berries, sure? –
Ah! that's the waiting maiden's joke, though looking so demure.

Frederick Barnard: The Cosy Old Maids' Christmas – ILN *1889 Christmas Supplement..*

Frederick Barnard: The Crusty Old Bachelors' Christmas – ILN 1889 Christmas Supplement.

There is, of course, an assumption that somehow or the other the ladies have private incomes.

The *Crusty Old Bachelors' Christmas* mocks their inability to live as cheerily as Misses B and C, and in doing so mocks, too, the continuing contemporary belief that women who failed to marry could not create a life of satisfying independence, and inevitably must become bitter and reclusive. Here it is the men who succumb and become crabbed, much like Marley and Scrooge. As they sit miserably and separately in a chop house, the crusty old bachelors' poem says:

Shame on you, grim old bachelors, who sit so moody there!
Why, don't you know it's Christmas Eve? Oh, you're a dismal pair!
Munching and tippling there alone, and gloating o'er stale news,
When you could be the central suns of merry, laughing crews

Consider the poor waiter, too, who longs to be away;
Tip him right well, and send him home a grateful man, and gay.
Throw down your papers, men alive! and keep no more apart;
Come, hob-a-nob! Ha, ha! where's now the ice within each heart?

Harry Furniss: A Happy Christmas in the Country – ILN *18 December 1880.*

A Happy Christmas in the Country

In December 1880 *A Happy Christmas in the Country* by the cartoonist Harry Furniss followed the fictional Titus Topsell as his ice-sailing machine landed him in trouble on a frozen lake but brought him the admiration of a fashionable young lady. Here a young man's fool-hardy spirit of adventure combined with the Victorian delight in modern technology provided an opportunity for romance to flourish despite, or perhaps because of, his embarrassing mishaps.

Not everything about this serial cartoon was fiction as ice yatching and ice-sailing machines were a reality in the late nineteenth century, especially in Canada and Scandinavia. However Topsell has added a jib-boom with sprit-sails and screw propellor thereby foolishly making the machine too powerful to control and he *is lifted up into the air, and is whirled away, over the meadows and hamlets of Frostyshire, till the winds lulls suddenly and drops him in somebody's private grounds.* He crashes into a tree, and from there falls head first through the ice on the pond where the Cutter family and their friends are skating. Skating was a popular Victorian pastime on the frozen lakes of landscaped estates. Fortunately Topsell knows the Cutters, and they care for him over Christmas, but as determined as ever he tries out his machine again this time with Miss Cutter alongside him. *They are a pair of rash young persons, and everyone knows what their fate is sure to be. "Of course they fall – in love."* Fortunately young Topsell came from a family with sufficient wealth to afford such a hobby, and sufficient social status to have acquired the friendship of the Cutters.

An English Christmas Depicted by a Japanese Artist

At first sight the serpentine cartoon (featured overleaf) *An English Christmas depicted by a Japanese artist*, cited as Kru-Shan-Ki, looked just like the title said. Appearing on Christmas Day 1880, the *ILN* asserted that *Since the recent and sudden increase of mercantile and social communications between England and Japan, the lively and intelligent people of that country have felt a great curiosity to learn all they can of our domestic manners, as well as our arts and sciences, our laws and public institutions. As European fashions of dress are now worn at the Mikado's Imperial Court, and carriages like ours have begun to supersede the palaquin or "norimon" and the "jin-rik-sha", the journalists, novelists, dramatists, and popular artists of Japan frequently amuse their public with pictures of English life.*

This was true. Japan had long resisted Western intervention in its affairs, but had little means of resisting the mix of the USA's naval might and aggressive diplomacy when it sought and secured trading agreements in 1853. Although there followed years of tension and outright conflict between Japanese forces of conservatism, notably the famed samurai and shogunate who had dominated the Imperial government for several centuries, the internal forces favouring change grew in influence until the young Emperor Meiji was able to subdue and abolish both the samurai and shogunate. By 1880 the modernisation of the government and economy was well underway.

The whole illustration, though, was a convoluted spoof by the well-known political and social satirist George Cruikshank (1842-1910), who styled himself 'Junior' and was the nephew of George Cruikshank (1792-1878), the more renowned political cartoonist of the same name. The illustration was less than complementary to Japanese artists and to the English capacity to enjoy themselves. One give-away was that the scenes were viewed clockwise from top left, unlike the Japanese custom of right to left. The 'Japanese' artist was congratulated *on the tolerably good notion of a Christmas Pantomime at one of our theatres.* The faces of the musicians and audience were *rendered with great powers of expression.* The *ILN* thought the artist must have seen an English kitchen to portray the making of the enormous Christmas pudding.

In the centre picture the family are eating Christmas dinner and the commentary mocked the cooked bird looking like a pelican and being far outweighed by the pudding. It thought *They are, one and all, making dreadful faces, as if the viands were uncommonly nasty. The Japanese may think so they are.* To the left of the central picture were two drawings of miserable people by themselves at Christmas, and to the right two others are having a better time, although the *ILN* mocked the idea of playing croquet at Christmas. The bottom two pictures featured a children's party with musical accompaniment and plenty of food, and then the children asleep.

Kru–Shan–Ki (George Cruikshank Jnr): An English Christmas depicted by a Japanese artist – ILN *25 December 1880.*

Frederick Barnard: The First Quadrille – ILN 13 December 1873.

The First Quadrille and
The Last Gallop

In December 1873 two pictures by Frederick Barnard (1846-96) entitled the *The First Quadrille* and *The Last Gallop* revealed the capacity of the Victorians, like any other generation, to take a risk, 'let go' and enjoy themselves – to the point of embarrassment – should the opportunity present itself. The illustrations recorded how dances tended to descend, or ascend, from cool decorum and rectitude at the start to a collective rousing pounding of the floor and a release of amorous feeling by the end. A lengthy poem by John Latey followed such a night of loosening behaviour and melting emotions. It starts with:

Precise and prim, demurely rigid,
With formal bows and curtsies frigid,
The first quadrille is gone through dumbly

Each partner setting, turning glumly,
As though, in his and her despite,
Performing some funereal rite.

Later things warm up.

But soon the spirit of the hour
Exerts o'er all its magic power.
In virtue of Dame Nature's law
Together youth and beauty draw.

The dances get faster, and then comes the Gallop.

So round and round, and to and fro,
Like dancing dervishes they go;
And chased and chasing ever flee
In giddy maze of ecstasy.
Yet damsels in their swiftest flight
Can shoot their Parthian arrows bright –
Keen arrows, tipped with pleasing pain –
Into the breast of passing swain.

Frederick Barnard: The Last Gallop – ILN 13 December 1873.

CHAPTER EIGHT

Christmas Trees, Christmas Presents and Christmas Cards: New Horizons

Christmas Trees

The Victorians took decorating fir trees to their hearts. Their origins are lost in the mists of time, but perhaps stem from the Christianisation of pagan Germanic tribes who had revered evergreen trees and shrubs as the symbol of eternal life. The custom, it is said, was strengthened among Protestants after the Reformation theologian Martin Luther (1483-1546) publicly attached candles to a fir tree, and possibly the practice acted as a decorative alternative to the cribs in Roman Catholic houses and churches. In Poland a pre-Christian tradition of hanging evergreen branches from the ceiling in mid-winter in the hope of a good harvest in the coming months survived to become a popular Christian habit. The practice of decorating trees spread cross northern Europe, and was taken abroad by emigrants. Many German and Baltic Hanseatic League merchants had well-established homes and businesses in Great Britain, and no doubt their families kept the tradition alive. Queen Charlotte, the German born wife of King George III, lit the candles on an indoor tree at a children's party in 1800, and when still a young princess in 1832, the future Queen Victoria recorded in her diary her joy at seeing two decorated trees surrounded by presents. Following Victoria's marriage to her cousin Prince Albert of Saxe-Coburg-Gotha in 1841, their enthusiasm for them led the Christmas tree to become popular among Britain's wealthier classes. As a novelty it possessed social cachet, it was something the whole family could enjoy, and it deliciously heightened children's anticipation of presents and parties.

In 1847 and 1848 the *ILN* featured the royal tree at Windsor Castle with the royal family gathered around. It epitomised the Victorian move towards making the family the centre of Christmas festivities. The ornate frame comprises vast quantities of fruit and game with medallions contrasting people shivering and begging alms while others are happily skating, enjoying a sleigh ride and warming themselves by a fire.

The Christmas Tree at Windsor Castle – ILN *1848 Christmas Supplement.*

The Gigantic Christmas Tree at the Crystal Palace

On 23 December 1854 the *ILN* featured the giant Christmas tree in the Crystal Palace, recently transferred to Sydenham from Hyde Park after the closure of the Great Exhibition. It reflected the Victorians inclination towards exuberance and fascination for the bizarre, and readiness to link anything with aggressive patriotism. The *stupendous festive trophy* soared high into the Central Transept, and was encircled by several smaller trees. *The monster Tree is loaded with a variety of brilliant ornaments and knickknacks, a profusion of large and small Chinese lanterns, and a number of flags and banners of all nations – the Turkish, supported by the French and English flags, occupying the top of the Tree.* The Crimean War was underway between these three countries and Imperial Russia, and the *ILN* acidly added, *The Holy Season breathes love and peace; but the Tree is made to bear "the very age and body of the time", by combining it with a group of glittering emblems of war.*

Below the great tree were grouped symbols of the Four Seasons, and plentiful examples of the taxidermist's art that so delighted the Victorians. *One of these groups contains two hares, two wood-pigeons, a brace of snipe, a pair of black grouse, a bittern, a sheldrake, and a pair of teal. Another has a turkey, two wild ducks, two golden plovers, two white hares, three red grouse, and two larks; a third displays a goose, three pheasants, a pair of red-legged partridges, a capercailzie, and a pewit; and the fourth, a swan, a pair of partridges, a pair of woodcocks, a pair of curlews, a guinea-fowl, two rabbits, and a pheasant of a new breed. The first specimens were shot a few days ago, and forwarded to her Majesty; and the one now at the Crystal Palace is the only other specimen of this rare bird which has ever been seen in this country.* Below and around the birds and animals were a variety of shrubs interspersed with flowers and fruit made out of coloured glass. A host of coal-fired factories were turning out such decorative items along with the glass perfume bottles, cake stands, vases and framed mirrors that were filling Victorian homes.

The Gigantic Christmas tree at the Crystal Palace – ILN 23 December 1854.

An Allegorical Tree

On 20 December 1856 another huge Christmas Tree appeared in the *ILN* but this time covered with human beings clambering over each other to get to the top. Towards the top choices had to be made. A spectral nativity scene hovered near a branch holding a Bible, opposite it a branch with leg-irons was overlooked by a devil, and at the very top hung an elusive crown. The artist was Henry Duff Linton (1815-99) and he portrayed a distinctly disturbing interpretation of the Tree of Life. It was accompanied by a cautionary poem whose condemnation of culpable excesses was a Christmas gift to anyone seeing only the worst in human nature. The author was Cuthbert Bede, otherwise the Revd Edward Bradley (1827-89), a Lincolnshire clergyman. Two of the verses read:

Here are Sin's masqueraders –
Wolves in the clothing of lambs –
In juggle and falsehood, traders,
Dealers in cheats and shams.
Onward they rush
With a riotous crush;
And, so that they reach the Tree's fair fruit,
They care not the axe is laid t the root.
Press on, ye rebel crew;
The prizes are all in view.

Avarice, Greed, and Fraud,
Forget that ye are brothers!
Clutch at each glittering gaud _
Mitre, and sceptre, and crown,
Sword, and jewel, and star,
Dangling above you they are –
Climb for them, tear them down!
Why should you leave them for others!

Henry Duff Linton: The Christmas Tree – ILN 20 December 1856.

The allegory ends with lines which, if taken literally, could easily sour any family's Christmas celebrations.

But you scorn to look
To the Saviour's Book,
And rush to the side, where the Devil
Looks down, with a grim delight,
On his children's maddening revel
On their chosen Christmas night.
For Satan hath hung his prizes
On the goodly Christmas Tree;
And there, in Sin's disguises,
Crowd the thoughtless company.

Christmas Presents around the Tree

Families and children, and an accumulation of presents, took centre-stage in Christmas tree illustrations from mid-century onwards. With gifts galore, it was an expensive trend, and not surprisingly illustrations reflect the comfortable middle classes. On Christmas Day 1858 James Abbot Pasquier (1826-84) featured a children's party from such a home as presents were being distributed around the tree. The toys included a Devil Mask, Noah's Ark, Punch, a drum, a ball, and a horse on wheels. One child looks as though she is taking part in a lucky dip.

The 1892 Christmas Supplement went further up-market with a picture by Amedee Forestier (1854-1930) of a country house reception where, with the superbly attired adults looking on, the equally well-dressed children were dancing around the tree prior to the presents being distributed. Forestier gave his picture the title *The Merry-Go-Round.* At first sight it referred solely to the dancing children, but with its tinge of superficiality and futility it could easily have referred to the constant round of dinners, dances and receptions these wealthy families attended in London and the country.

Amedee Forestier: The Merry–Go–Round – ILN 1892 Christmas Supplement.

James Abbot Pasquier: The Christmas Tree – ILN 25 December 1858.

Hoisting the Union Jack

An illustration by Alfred Hunt (1830-96) in the 1876 Christmas Supplement featured a wealthy family amid its Christmas luxury. Everyone is well-dressed, and the decorations and presents are abundant. However among the numerous toys and baubles there are several small figures with less than friendly faces much like those in many Victorian illustrations of fairies and elves (see pages 150-163). Perhaps it was the whim of the artist, and perhaps linked to the contemporary fascination with the supernatural and bizarre, and the undercurrents of Victorian unease at the alleged triumph of greed and materialism over religious belief.

However, the title of Hunt's picture is *Hoisting the Union Flag*, and it is particularly significant that the mother is helping her young son place what looks like the Blue Ensign (and not the Union Jack) at the top of the tree. He is wearing the knee-length petticoats of boys until they were 'breeched' around the age of three or four. The youngest daughter is wearing a miniature and shorter version of an adult's outfit. Their mother is the devoted supporter of the men in her household, and notably of their roles in always acting honourably while also protecting the nation and extending the Empire. The accompanying poem sees the boy as a future soldier, and as the flag is placed his mother says:

"Now, Poppet, firm and steady!:
Well done, my darling Freddy!
Aim high, and strike for right, by deed and tongue and pen,
Despite all scorn and laughter,
Throughout your whole hereafter!"
Thus spake the fair young mother; the father cried, "Amen".

The flag is a little confusing. Until 1864 the Red, White and Blue ensigns were flown by the Red, White and Blue squadrons respectively of the Royal Navy, but after that date the White Ensign (with its red cross covering the whole flag) was reserved for warships, the Red Ensign for merchant vessels, and the Blue Ensign for merchant and national vessels crewed by retired Royal Navy officers or reservists. Perhaps the artist had forgotten the changes, or the flag referred to an historic battle in which an ancestor of the family had fought.

Another two verses summarise the growing Victorian inclination to place the wife and mother on a daunting, almost sacred, pedestal of feminine and domestic virtues as the prime mover of family stability and happiness. Her approval of her menfolk's careers, patriotism, integrity and valour was important.

O Home! celestial focus!
By some sweet hocus-focus
All low thoughts in you die, and noble ones have birth;
In your transfiguring splendour
Of love's glad self-surrender
Home seems a gleam of heaven flashed on this planet earth.

Who but a wife and mother
Befits this home? None other.
To heaven's viceregent ever the household all incline –
However fluctuating,
Around her gravitating,
As planets round the sun, in harmony divine.

Alfred Hunt: Hoisting the Union Jack – ILN 1876 Christmas Supplement.

Advertisements for Christmas Presents

As the early Christmas tree illustrations reveal, the giving of presents to family, and maybe friends, was becoming increasingly fashionable, especially in the second half of the century. In earlier times, Boxing Day had been the traditional day for presents, but not generally to the family. For many centuries gifts to the poor had been placed in alms boxes in churches, and special church offerings had been made on Saint Stephen's Day which in western Europe was always the day after Christmas Day. And as early as 1663 Samuel Pepys noted in his diary that on the next working day to Christmas Day tradesmen hoped for 'Christmas Boxes' of money in gratitude for good services during the year, and the custom has been long lasting. Servants, too, came to expect presents.

On 16 December 1843 the *ILN* contained a few small advertisements seizing the growing habit of present-giving as a commercial opportunity. Cornwall & Co. in Walbrook, London, offered Christmas hampers of a dozen bottles of Champagne, Bucellas, Crusted Port or Sherry for 7 guineas, and John Sweeting of Cheapside offered *Barrelled Oysters for Christmas* from his English stock – reassuringly *not Scotch, Welch, or French* – that arrived each morning by train. In the same edition James Burns of London listed twenty books as suitable Christmas and New Year's gifts ranging from *Eastern Romance (Tales of the Arabian Nights)* and *Popular Tales & Legends* to *Scripture History for Children* and *Australia Properly Described*, and the entrepreneur John Joseph Mechi offered *Unique Christmas Presents* that turned out to be his usual range of ladies cabinets, jewel boxes, small tables and dressing cases.

Dr Richter's Expeller advertisement – ILN 24 November 1888. Friedrich Richter was a quack who made a fortune from his pain 'expeller' which was a mix of peppers, herb oils and dried rhatany and galangal roots.

By the 1880s December editions contained several pages of fully illustrated Christmas advertisements, some a costly half a page or more in size. The range of goods was vast, and unsurprisingly so since mass production techniques enabled the middle class Victorian house to be filled with an unprecedented array of furniture, fittings, gadgets and ornaments, and many Victorians were eager to purchase them to display their social status. Advertisers were adept at attaching seasonal images to their goods. In 1888 the Magi pointing to the Star arriving over Bethlehem heralded Dr Richter's Expeller, an embrocation that cured nearly everything, including, miraculously, influenza. And in the same year Punchinello advertised Parkins & Gotto's toys, and John Brinsmead & Sons sought to sell pianos by showing several men in evening dress admiring an elegant young women playing one at a seasonal reception. In 1890 a happy smiling face of Father Christmas (the American import) advertised *Parkins & Gotto's 10,000 Xmas Presents,* and a wealthy young lady on a seasonal errand of mercy carried Fry's Cocoa prominently in her basket as a gift to the needy. The Vinolia Company of Bond Street had been founded in

1885 and placed great reliance on its eye catching packaging and variety of seasonal advertisements to market its products.

Parkins & Gotto advertisement – ILN 24 November 1888. The company flourished in the second half of the nineteenth century selling stationery, luggage, leather goods and sports equipment.

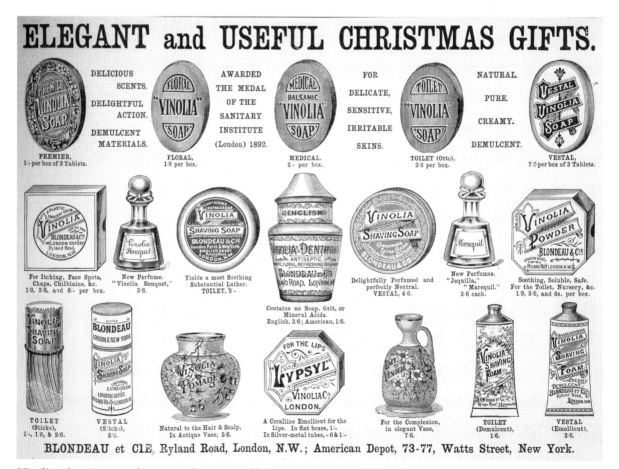

Vinolia advertisement for men and women's Christmas presents – ILN 24 December 1892.

The Toy Stalls of Lowther Arcade

On Christmas Eve 1870 the *ILN* pictured the crowded toy stalls in London's Lowther Arcade. It trumpeted the achievement of toy manufacturers, advertisers and retailers, and the success of turning Christmas into a festival increasingly targeting children – at least those in families with money to spend on them. The illustration by Charles Joseph Staniland (1838-1916) featured excited children and their indulgent parents and grandparents amidst the traders and their array of enticing toys.

The commentary, though, gives this happy if indulgent scene a typically unsettling Victorian 'spin'. *As Christmas approaches, broughams and cabs may be seen at the principal toy marts pouring out groups of excited boys and girls, who presently return with their arms full of playthings and the oddest articles which the ingenuity of man can devise and the wealth of parents and friends can buy. The boys are mostly laden with warriors armed cap-a-pie, drums, trumpets, blunderbusses, and grotesque, horrid-looking demons, which grin and roll their eyes in the ghastliest manner; while the young ladies, as becomes the gentler sex, generally choose what is graceful and dainty, having keen eyes for the useful as well as the ornamental.*

Lowther Arcade was built in 1830 and ran from the Strand to Adelaide Street. It housed 24 shops which by the 1840s were leased by a variety of toy manufacturers from across Europe and the USA. It was immensely popular, but was demolished in 1902 to make way for the new Coutts Bank building.

Charles Joseph Staniland: Lowther Arcade at Christmas Time – ILN 24 December 1870.

The Post Office & Christmas Cards

An article on 19 December 1886 highlighted the mounting pressure on the Post Office at Christmas, and notably on Christmas Eve, the day on which the greatest number of cards and packages were posted, and on Christmas Day, when they were expected to be delivered. It said over 50,000,000 items were anticipated that Christmas, and this easily outstripped the number of St Valentine's Day cards posted in February. During Christmas week at London's main Post Office at St Martins-le-Grand 3,000 staff worked *stamping, sorting, carrying, bundling, bagging, tying and sealing as if for dear life's sake. The actual struggle may be said to commence on the morning of Dec. 23, and is at its fiercest on the 24th, when hardly any of the officials are allowed to leave the office.....the struggle continues, with almost unabated vigour until far into Christmas Day, as the correspondence pours in until late at night.... The work does not actually cease until about ten o'clock on Christmas morning, when the officials are allowed to go home.*

Of the postman's share in the Christmas work there is but little need to to speak, so well acquainted with it everyone must be. His is a familiar figure, and, indeed, prominent feature of Christmas morn, as he pursues his "walk", sinking under a load of congratulations, wishes, greetings, and friendly messages; and so thoroughly well able are the public to sympathise with the arduousness of his labours that he is probably the only person to whom the customary Christmas box is given without regret or murmur. So popular, indeed, are the postmen, that the Postmaster-General is constrained to issue a notice urging the public not to offer them drink on Christmas Day, an act of mistaken kindness, of which too many, we are afraid, are prone to be guilty.

After a slow start the sale of Christmas cards had soared from the 1860s onwards. The first card was produced in 1843 for Henry Cole (later Sir Henry) (1808-82) from a design by John Hallcott Horsley, but as each one cost a hefty shilling Cole's imaginative venture led to only modest sales. Cole's own future was bright, though, as he was instrumental alongside Prince Albert in staging the 1851 Great Exhibition and became the first director of the Victoria & Albert Museum built

Christmas Card – author's collection.

New Year's Card – author's collection.

from its profits. Nevertheless Christmas cards became increasingly popular as advances in colour lithograph printing lowered the cost, with images of animals, flowers and children being popular, and, perhaps surprisingly, images of winter and the Nativity far less so. The enticing prospect of a sunny Spring seems to have outshone any enjoyment of a freezing cold winter.

Humorous pictures were popular too, although some had that streak of morbidity, fear or cruelty to be seen in Victorian stories and pantomimes deemed appropriate for family consumption. Two examples pictured here (not in the *ILN*) had children plucking a live turkey, and boys throwing snowballs causing a man to spill the Christmas dinner he had just collected from the baker's oven (see also illustration on page 42).

Among many other examples, some cards featured insects such as stag beetles and cockroaches, and animals such as cats, frogs and rats, bizarrely dressed as humans playing games, dancing and eating meals.

Louis Wain: A Cat's Party – ILN 27 December 1890. Louis Wain (1860–1939) was particularly renowned for his numerous illustrations of anthropomorphised cats.

Somewhat uneasily to modern eyes, on occasion these often overbearing creatures were pictured the size of children, and playing with or chasing them. Others had children gripping spoons and forks chasing a Christmas pudding that possessed human features, or children literally diving into whole puddings.

On 13 December 1884 an *ILN* article on the popularity of Christmas cards recorded that *Purchasers old and young, men, women, and children, are seen to crowd the shop-windows and shop-counters of enterprising fancy-stationers, and there are situations amidst the eager throng when height is an advantage enabling the taller person to look over the others' heads, and to pick up the article of his choice. Where the bustle of buying is so great, it may happen that some impatience is felt at the tedious procedure of the elderly spinster who insists on a critical perusal of all the printed text on every card offered to her inspection.*

Although German inspired Christmas cards showing *Krampus*, the long tongued black horned goat of northern European legend seeking out little children ostensibly to befriend but actually to judge and possibly whip even kill, for misbehaviour, may have filtered into Great Britain, the *ILN* made no mention of these deeply disturbing images (at least to modern eyes). It reserved its adverse comments for the fad of mocking *"personality cards" which circulate pictorial and epigrammatic pasquinades against people one meets in society.*

When cheap Christmas postcards with a ha'penny postage were introduced in 1870 they rapidly outstripped the card in an envelope and its penny postage. Thomas Chapman of Leicester Square took out large scale advertisements in the *ILN* in the 1880s and onwards detailing a huge range of cards at varying prices, some with religious connections but the great majority were about the natural world and famous paintings. Among Chapman's boxed sets for 1884 there were those featuring winsome or alarming children such as *Young Girls, Girlish Beauties, Winter Pastimes, Quaint Children* and *Destructive Babies,* or flowers such as *Rose Blossoms* and *Heather Bells,* and animals such as *Bird Studies, Hunting, House Dogs, Robins in Groups, Deer, Swans, Storks, Squirrels* and *Monkeys.* There was always room, though, for the popular *Animated Vegetables,* and supernatural world of *Fairy Land* and *Sea Sprites.*

BLESSINGS ATTEND THEE THROUGHOUT THE YEAR.

Christmas card from a House Dogs set c1880 – author's collection.

134

CHAPTER NINE

The Evolution of Pantomimes: Worlds of Wild Imagination

Christmas Entertainment in Transition

In the 1840s British pantomimes were in a lengthy period of transition towards the modern telling of a colourful fairy tale or fable interspersed with songs, slapstick humour and topical jokes. In the eighteenth and early nineteenth centuries their predecessors were very different. They contained an eclectic mix of elements, some drawn from Classical plays or the old mummers' plays with their fantastic creatures, fights, gender role reversal and theme of good conquering evil, and some imported from overseas, notably the celebrated Harlequinade from Italy.

In England the Harlequinade became a popular standard element which centred upon the lovers Harlequin and Columbine eloping and being pursued by Columbine's angry and avaricious father, Pantaloon, and his comic henchmen, Clown and Pierrot. The cast always wore traditionally styled costumes easily recognisable as the character they were playing. The excitement for the audience lay in novelty of the lovers' many scrapes and escapes. Harlequin was romantic and mercurial, with a tight fitting diamond patterned outfit. Columbine was a devoted but often frightened lover and her dress usually included a white cap and apron. The Clown, whose tricks hindered the chase rather than hastening it, was dressed garishly with ruff and tassels. The avaricious and sometimes cruel Pantaloon traditionally had a red jacket and trousers, a skullcap, hooked nose and grey beard, and Pierrot, often serving as Pantaloon's servant and rather in love with Columbine himself, had a serious white face and predominantly white clothing. In due course an inept policeman was often added to the cast – a shrewd move as Sir Robert Peel's new police force for London created in 1829 was viewed by many as over-zealous and an unwelcome threat to personal liberty.

Usually these entertainments started with a play which was followed by a comic Harlequinade – both of which until the law changed in 1843 had to be played in mime with musical accompaniment – often in halls attached to public houses. The1737 Licensing Act had limited spoken drama to the 'patent theatres' – the Theatre Royals in Drury Lane and Covent Garden. However after 1843 the Lord Chamberlain could only ban plays likely to offend decency and disturb public order. Magistrates could licence many more premises, and as a result many more purpose built theatres were built.

The connection between the play and the Harlequinade was minimal. Gradually, though, the early nineteenth century saw the plays being replaced by themes developed out of fairy tales, fables and folk tales, but always with a Harlequinade as an important and separate second part. This led to the practice of giving many shows dual titles, such as *Harlequin and Johnny Gilpin's Ride, Harlequin and Robinson Crusoe*, and *Harlequin and Crotchet & Quaver*, all of which were staged in December 1844. The next change was for the fairy stories to be linked more closely with the Harlequinade, so that the lovers and their parents could be magically transformed by a fairy godmother into the Harlequinade for the build up of adventures leading to the increasingly elaborately staged denouement. The greater freedom allowed in 1843 gave a great boost to writers and producers, as did the trend for pantomimes to become a popular Christmas-time family outing, usually from Boxing Day onwards. Many theatres invested heavily in new pantomimes, seeing them as the major profit-making productions of the year.

The fairy godmother begins the Harlequinade at the City of London Theatre – ILN *2 January 1847.*

As the second half of the century progressed the importance of the Harlequinade faded. Although audiences expected it to appear, many of its antics were absorbed into pantomimes that significantly extended the fairy and folk tale elements. The range of stories was huge, with new ones tried out every year, and far more adventurous than the safe themes modern productions tend to select. This was primarily the work of two writers, Henry James Byron (1835-84) and James Planche (1796-1880), and the Drury Lane Theatre manager/producer Sir Augustus Harris (1852-96). Harris led the way in staging costly pantomimes, full of music hall stars, dozens of dancers and extras, huge orchestras, and magical set pieces, that subsidised the more serious productions during the rest of the year.

Cat's Castle or Harlequin and the King of the Rats

On 28 December 1844 the *ILN* noted the dual titles of most pantomimes, and its reports highlighted the magical transition of the initial characters into those of the Harlequinade, usually just over half way though the performance, One was the unusual *Cat's Castle or Harlequin and the King of the Rats* at the Adelphi Theatre. Princess Molrow is the daughter of King Whiskers of the Rats whose Generalissimo, Killcat, has been ordered to prepare for war against the Kingdom of the Felines where abides Prince Tortoiseshell Tom who (clearly against type) has fallen in love with the rat princess. Much of the action occurs during the build-up to the battle for Cat's Castle where the brave defenders include Colonel Purwell and Major Fitz-spit. The castle is spectacularly destroyed, and then Fairy Honeysuckle equally spectacularly transforms Molrow and Tortoiseshell Tom into Columbine and Harlequin, and Whiskers and Killcat to Clown and Pantaloon. The adventures of the lovers are set within a series of *dioramic tableaux* recalling real events in 1844 such as the construction of Brunel's Hungerford Suspension Bridge across the Thames, the visit of the diminutive American circus performer 'General Tom Thumb', the *Running Rein* fraud (when the Derby winner was not *Running Rein*, the horse officially entered for the race), and the new and greatly mocked 'Wash-houses for the Industrious Classes'.

Scene from 'Cat's Castle or Harlequin and the King of the Rats' at the Adelphi Theatre, London – ILN 28 December 1844.

Henry Vizetelly: Pantomime Night – ILN *8 January 1848.*

The Audience

At the height of the pantomime season in January 1848 the *ILN* entertained readers with the artist Henry Vizetelly's (1820-94) perception of audiences occupying the variously priced seats. The illustration highlighted the relative decorum of the boxes, and the crush, noise and bustle in the gallery and pit, as people laughed, shouted out, ate and drank, and annoyed those next to them. It was accompanied by an article by the *ILN*'s regular humorist Angus Reach (1821-56). He noted that the adults in the expensive boxes, whatever their elevated station in life, succumb to the humour as much as their children. Picking on one, he said that *you have, sir, roared out an incontrollable guffaw, as you beheld that most felonious-minded of clowns steal a poker, and then thoughtlessly and culpably insinuate the red hot end into his venerable friend Pantaloon's capacious pockets. And the old boys – ay, and the old girls – are just as happy as the young ones.*

Reach said two types of people occupied the pit: those who lounged around in the lobbies, sauntered in for a particular scene, chattered during the performance while closely inspecting *the beauties of their fair neighbours,* and those who got every pennyworth of their 3/-d seat by storming their way to the front, and steadfastly ignoring every distraction.

The gallery, he asserted, is a *chaos of struggling arms and legs, and grimy, grinning features – and ginger beer bottles that do not hold ginger-beer, but something stronger – and half-smashed straw-bonnets fastened to the brass stancheons – and shirt sleeves – and half-sucked oranges – and thick sandwiches – and perspiring public house boys, struggling through dense rows of humanity with tin pails, and keeping up a monotonous howl of "potaw, gents – potaw – potaw, gents".* ('Potaw' was porter, a brown ale that was gradually replaced in popularity by 'mild'.)

However changes were afoot. The relaxation of the licensing laws in 1843 led to new theatres and innovative productions with sumptuous scenery and exciting stunts competing for custom. The old customs of well-lit audiences was replaced by

John Leech: Going to the pantomime – ILN *24 December 1853.*

darkened auditoriums and well lit stages, and shrewd seat pricing within the new purpose-built theatres kept the social classes largely apart in side boxes, dress circles and stalls. Gradually too, the custom of incredibly lengthy productions – some four or five hours long involving several 'pieces' – was replaced by more unified shows of specific genres. However as late as 7 January 1882 the *ILN* complained that the impressive but relentless spectacles of *Little Bo Peep* at Covent Garden lasting three hours and twenty minutes badly needed *the relief and a boon* of two intervals. Increasingly, though, everyone was treating the theatre as a place to see productions of one's choice rather than a public house, chop-house, meeting place, and hawking place for prostitutes that also offered plays one may or may not really want to see.

Going to the Pantomine

On Christmas Eve 1853 an illustration by the cartoonist John Leech (1817-64) showed a portly gentleman following his equally portly wife into a carriage on an evening out to a pantomime with their numerous children. Rather disparagingly the commentary thought he was a wholesale grocer, but nevertheless wealthy enough to be *a citizen of credit and renown.* Two children's nurses are in attendance, a second carriage lies ready to take on board some of the children, and a delivery boy looks on. The commentary strongly implies they were just the uncritical but wealthy audience pantomime producers were looking for to fill the over-priced boxes.

Rehearsals

The vast number of people required for Victorian Christmas productions meant that performers outside the main characters were hired just as rehearsals began. It seems there was no shortage of applicants. In December 1858 the *ILN* described the crowd pushing at the doors of Drury Lane. *Such was the state of emulation, the pressure, and the crush, that it was necessary to call in the aid of the police....But nothing will do. Grown man and woman, and ambitious urchin, not unprotected or unencouraged by his female guardian, are still resolute to earn their shilling and eighteenpence each per night, and are not a little riotous in their demand. We trust that the management has made a judicious selection from the throng, and that many who were deserving have benefited by the occasion.* The *ILN* said these crowds reflected *the great amount of the surplus population, and give evidence that greater numbers are willing to work than can get work to do.* (Quote: *ILN* 25 December 1858)

On Boxing Day 1868 an action-packed picture by an unnamed artist showed the hectic preparations underway for a major pantomime. The *ILN* said *it shows a bit of the inner life of the stage, the drilling the youths and maidens who contribute so largely to the fun and the grace of the spectacles which are now in full swing. The process is one which requires patience and painstaking, especially with the masculine recruits, girls always learning everything much more quickly than the stupider sex. It may be mentioned, also, that as the remuneration given to this class of artist is not very large, it is naturally supplied from the not very cultivated portion of the population.*

Boy by boy has to be vigilantly watched, and it has to be made perfectly clear to his possibly not overly lucid mind exactly what he is to do.....He has also to be taught presence of mind , and to know that if the clown or pantaloon is seized with an unusual access of vigour and happens to knock him about a little, he is not to be frightened, or to howl, as his instinct might prompt, far less is he to try to get out of the way.

Girls like the work, they are made to look as pretty as possible, and they know that they will be admired, more or less....But, in any case, the drill is frequent and severe; and the audiences who applaud the gaily-dressed and adroit creatures who perform before them know little how many hours of labour and practice are represented by a scene or a dance, and do not know that the artists have most likely walked long distances to rehearsals, probably in bad weather, and that, after protracted exercise, they have to walk home again, weary and hungry, and seldom to any luxurious meal.

Preparing for the pantomime at a London theatre – ILN 26 December 1868.

'Valentine & Orson' at Covent Garden

On New Year's Day 1881 a series of drawings portrayed the rehearsals at Covent Garden Theatre for the now forgotten pantomime *Valentine and Orson*. This was based upon a medieval French romance about twin brothers who were abandoned in a forest as babies. Valentine is found and raised as an honoured knight at the court of Pepin, the eighth century King of the Franks, while Orson grows up in a den of bears and becomes a wild man of the woods. He is overcome and tamed by Valentine, whose friend he becomes, and eventually their true history is revealed by a magical bronze head. The pair then set off to rescue their mother Bellisant, who is the sister of Pepin, from the thrall of the giant Ferragus into whose hands she had fallen after being repudiated by her husband, an Eastern potentate.

Preparing for the pantomime 'Valentine & Orson' – ILN 1 January 1881.

The drawings show a couple of magical stage tricks, actors learning how to be animals and wear the giant's head, and a group of hired hands irritating their trainer by failing to march like soldiers.

As the first night neared – *Carpenters in gangs, and all under subordinate command, are ready at the ropes that would puzzle an experienced Jack Tar; scene shifters are watching with eager attention for their signal; fairies and amazons are edging their way through the crowd to be strapped on to the irons, or to fall into their ranks, and in every available corner there is wonderful medley of animals, birds, beasts, fishes, dancers, and peripatetic toys..... The ballet girls have been drilled and trained at some school removed from the theatre; and the band has practised in some deserted music room.... And children who, with all deference to the School Boards, know little of their mother tongue, are taught to speak intelligently, to pronounce clearly, and to sing in tune, to say nothing of an invaluable lesson in precision and deportment.* The swipe at the School Boards – the state and rate funded elementary schools that complemented the Anglican and Nonconformist schools – was largely unfair as spelling, handwriting, diction, and singing were important.

Katti Lanner

Katti Lanner (1829-1908) was the daughter of Joseph Lanner, a celebrated Viennese composer and director of dance music at the Imperial Austrian court. She was a talented ballet dancer, and became a choreographer. In the mid 1860s she founded a ballet school and troupe which toured Europe and North America to rapturous acclaim. In 1875 she settled in London to direct the National Training School for Dancing at Drury Lane and over the next decade she supervised many productions at the Theatre Royal, including pantomime routines. In 1887 she started a twenty year career as ballet mistress at Leicester Square's Empire Theatre of Varieties.

In January 1884 the *ILN* praised the Drury Lane School for the physical and mental stimulation of its training. In excess of eighty children were enrolled at any one time. They trained from 12.30pm until 2.00pm each day to enable them to attend ordinary schools as required by law – although the law at this date said they could leave at the age of 10 or 11 if they had reached a basic stage of literacy and numeracy. The training

Sketches at a training school for stage dancing – ILN 5 January 1884.

was free with costs being taken from the children's earnings on stage and the residue handed to the children's parents. Children attended daily and, said the *ILN, Big elder sisters, aunts, mothers and fathers wait for them at the theatre, and as soon as their little parts are over muffle them up and take them home. And how welcome their earnings are in many a family only those who are the true friends of the poor know.*

The Burlesque Heads

On 17 December1870 an illustration showed elaborate helmets and huge burlesque masks being made. *The moulder or painter of grotesque masks should be gifted with imagination and humour in a high degree, as well as great knowledge of the effects produced at a certain distance, by particular combinations of shapes and strong colours, under a glaring artificial light. His memory should be fully stored with the details of forcible physiognomy and antiquated or barbarian costume gathered from pictures of mankind in all nations of the world and in all ages of history or romance; his business is to see how these may be used in the queerest fresh combinations.*

Alfred Crowquill's 'A Dream of Chancifancia'

A week later, on Christmas Eve 1870, a fantasy montage by Alfred Crowquill featured many pantomime masks and costumes adorning curious and grotesque creatures, some human, others anthropomorphic animals, fish, insects and toys. The micro-scenes within the picture slide between delightful images of courtly musicians and lovers to potentially terrifying figures of a Harlequinade about to be swallowed by a giant fish, ballet dancers dangerously near a monstrous gaping head, and a birdlike figure grasped tightly in a giant hand.

There was a centuries-old tradition of entertainments such as masques and mummers' plays embracing the 'grotesque' and the 'fantastic'. Often called 'grotesque', the humanoid natural creatures and other supernatural beings who inhabited pantomimes, illustrated stories, and Christmas cards were part of the fusion of the familiar and alien, and the terrifying and comic, that fascinated many Victorians. They enjoyed the huge pantomime masks because they were

The Burlesque heads – ILN *17 December 1870.*

essentially caricatures of people, just as they were thrilled by the creation of 'fantastic' villains. They relished, too, the shock of macabre going-ons in ruined abbeys, castle dungeons and dark forests that filled stories from the tintillating Gothic novels to the 'penny dreadfuls', and they shivered in delight at the shock of sudden scene changes in pantomimes from light to darkness – anything, in fact, that created a sense of ominous tension and foreboding. The Victorians, though, did not shy aware from cruelty and death in their pantomimes, nor in their books for children where very often dire penalties awaited those straying from the path of virtue and goodness. With reference to modern definitions of cruelty, it was only during the lives of many Victorians that executions in public were ended, flogging with a cat-of-nine-tails in the army and navy ceased, the insane stopped being objects of entertainment for visitors, and the first attempts were made to protect child workers. Perhaps one way of dealing with the uncertainties and harshness of life, and the suddenness of death in many Victorian families, was to turn it into melodrama, fantasy, even comedy.

Alfred Crowquill: Gathering for the pantomime: A Dream of Chancifancia – ILN 24 December 1870.

Two Popular Themes

Two illustrations from 10 January 1874 identify two major trends. These were the inclusion of jokes about current affairs and spectacular dramatic surprises. Two of the background figures in *Jack in the Box* at Drury Lane feature the large heads of two high profile political rivals – Benjamin Disraeli, the Conservative Prime Minister, 1868 and 1874-80, and William Gladstone, the Liberal Prime Minister 1868-74 and 1880-85. A fortnight after this edition the expected general election replaced Gladstone by Disraeli as Prime Ministe. Pantomimes did not hesitate to caricature notable people, and and a variety of post holders such as beadles, school teachers, policemen and judges were commonly mocked in set scenes.

The dramatic scene from *Red Riding Hood and her sister Little Bo-Peep* epitomises the customary large casts of extras, awesome displays of epic scenery and provision of frightening moments. It also highlights the Victorian penchant for the supernatural and tragic. This is the "Lily Dell in the Glow-worm Vale", the home of the troupe of beautiful elves, but also the the haunt of a voracious dragon. Fulfilling his tragic destiny Marmion, the bother of Red Riding Hood, wounds the wolf that has pursued her here, but in offending the fairy law by drawing blood in the enchanted dell his heroism must, and does, result in his death.

'Jack in the Box' at Drury Lane Theatre – ILN 10 January 1874.

'Red RidingHood and her sister Little Bo–Peep' at Covent Garden Theatre – ILN 10 January 1874.

145

The Vokes Family

Magical surprises, humanised animals and humour with a decidedly cruel edge were the order of the day. On 5 January 1884 the *ILN* reported: *At Her Majesty's Theatre, by the aid of the popular Vokes family, and other clever performers, the old story of "Red Riding Hood" is presented with great animation; and the scene in which one person is transformed into a wolf, another into a fox, and a third into an ape, by the stroke of the enchanter's wand, is managed with remarkable skill; but the making of the wonderful rabbit-pie, and boiling the old lady in her own scullery copper, are somewhat too prolonged.*

The Vokes family of three sisters, Jessie (1848-84), Victoria (1853-94) and Rosina (1854-94), their brother Frederick (1846-88) and the actor Walter Fawdon (1844-1904) who assumed the name Vokes, were immensely popular pantomime and burlesque stars in London and the USA in the later 1860s and throughout the 1870s. After 1884 the family's reputation started to fade with Jessie's death that year, growing criticisms of their routines as out-of-date, and arguments with Augustus Harris, the influential impresario and stage-manager of Drury Lane Theatre, the scene of their greatest pantomime triumphs.

The Vokes family in Dick Whittington and his Cat – ILN 8 January 1876.

In January 1876 the family were to be seen at the height of their fame as actors and dancers in *Dick Whittington and his Cat* at Drury Lane. The *ILN* reported, *Here they are all in full action: Frederick Vokes as Master Fitzwilliam worried by the feline Tommy, Walter Vokes, but using his remarkable legs in the way of defence against the awkward attack of the irrepressible cat: Rosina Vokes as Alice Fitzwilliam and Victoria Vokes as her lover Dick, and the fairy Blue Bell (possibly Jessie) rendering supernatural aid to the faithful couple.*

Ali Baba & the Forty Thieves

Drury Lane Theatre's 1886-7 production of *Ali Baba & the Forty Thieves* probably represented the apogee of Victorian pantomime entertainment in terms of pageantry, music, dancing, star performances and, above, all never-ending surprises. 1887 was the year of Queen Victoria's Golden Jubilee, and the entertainment ensured this was celebrated along with the British Empire which was, rather belatedly, catching the public imagination.

The key-note of Mr. Augustus Harris's superlatively beautiful pantomime is struck in the very opening scene, a radiant "Peep at Paradise", gay with pretty faces and graceful forms, bedight in charming silks and satins, and closing with an inspiriting chorus. The adventures proper of Ali Baba and the Forty Thieves take place without and within the "Mystic Cavern", and in the enriched Ali's Palace; and are diversified by the droll tricks of the accomplished donkey (skilfully impersonated by Mr. Charles Lauri, jun.) and a wonderfully realistic monkey, evidently studied from nature by Mr. Paul Martinetti. This friendly pair caused infinite amusement by clambering up the private boxes, and by making the tour of the dress circle… As a troupe of diminutive monkeys, and a band of little dancers in white, the juvenile pupils of Madame Katti Lanner once again gained applause by their agile manoeuvres….But Mr.

Harris reserved his full strength for the dazzling processions, in the marshalling of which he has justly earned a great reputation for expert generalship. Marvellously dazzling as are the costly costumes worn by the battalions of brightly apparelled thieves in the Cavern, they are eclipsed by the imposing display in the Grand Jubilee processions which take the place of the ordinary transformation. Commencing with an allegory of the conquest of India, this splendid crowning effect comprises a processional and choreographic gathering of the clans which go to make up the British Empire, and ends with a gorgeous ballet in front of a large statue of her Majesty executed by Miss Mary Telbin, and with the singing of Mr. Clement Scott's Jubilee Ode to the Queen.

This was not the end. The Harlequinade followed with Ali Baba and Morgiana and the thieves pursued in a chase possessing both hilarious and nerve-tingling moments by the usual villains and a whole corps of inept police until the long expected happy ending.

Charles Lauri became famous as an animal impersonator, Paul Martinetti was a popular comic, William and Mary Telbin were noted set designers, and Clement Scott was a writer, and theatre critic much feared for his acerbic comments.

Henry Stephen (Hal) Ludlow (1861-c1934): Ali Baba & the Forty Thieves – ILN 1 January 1887.

Clowns

Several Victorian pantomime clowns became famous, and none more so than Harry Payne (1833-95) who featured in a series of comic pranks drawn by the eminent cartoonist Phil May (1864-1903) for the *ILN*'s 2 January 1892 edition. His brother Frederick Payne (1841-80) had often appeared as Harlequin alongside him until his early death. Clowns had easily recognisable costumes, and yet possessed complex characters. They could be clumsy and inept, and yet full of inventive mischief and clever tricks. Much of their success lay in their ability to create a sympathetic rapport with the audience, humiliate foolish or pompous characters, sometimes using surprisingly cruel jokes, and yet portray an element of inner sadness that belied their extrovert exterior. In many ways you never knew where you were with Clowns. Their characters could change disconcertingly in a blink of an eye.

The cartoons were taken from the pantomime at Drury Lane Theatre. In line one, Harry Payne clumsily hits a wicket-keeper and empties his pot on a couple of children. In line two the Harlequin uses magic to slam down the ticket office's shutter on the fingers of the Clown and Pantaloon for some trick they are playing. Line three featured the celebrated red-hot poker, with no doubt the Clown persuading the audience to encourage his cruel joke. Lines four, five and six tell the story of a dramatic illusion in which the Clown and Pantaloon blow up a policeman and piece him him back together – only for him to arrest them.

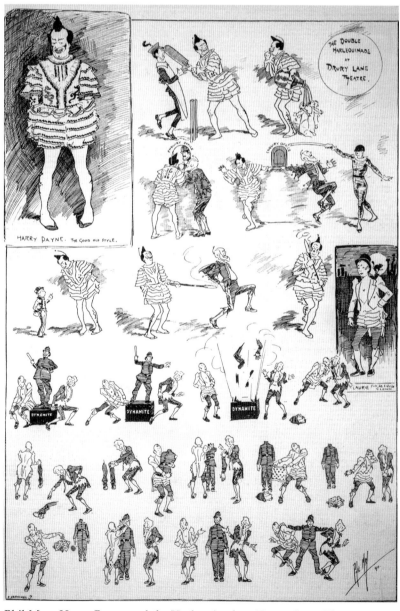

Phil May: Harry Payne and the Harlequinade at Drury Lane Theatre – ILN 2 January 1892.

Foundling Girls & Cinderella

An illustration on Christmas Day 1886 by Marcella Walker (fl. 1872-1917) featured two girls who probably never saw a pantomime but still had dreams of a richer life both emotionally and materially. Here both girls are lost in thought – one as she reads the story of Cinderella, and the other fondling a sprig of mistletoe. Pointedly the ILN asks:

Are these girls orphans? Are their parents dead?
Beat nowhere some young hearts with kindred blood?
Alas! they know not. Want, or Shame, has hidden
Their birth and family. Let this be said–
Kind Captain Coram, by Christ's Spirit bidden,
Built them a Home. God saw that it was good.

They were inmates of the renowned Foundling Hospital established with a Royal Charter in 1739 by Captain Thomas Coram (c1668-1751), a shipwright, sailor and merchant. Mothers unable to care for their babies left them at the Hospital, but also left a token that would identify the children should they ever be in a position to reclaim them. Foster families looked after the babies until the age of five when they were brought to the Hospital to be cared for and educated until the age of fifteen when many were apprenticed prior to going into various trades, domestic service or the armed forces. The Foundling Hospital caught the imagination of many socially and politically influential families, including George Frederic Handel, William Hogarth and Charles Dickens, and prospered with their support despite the intermittent scandals.

Marcella Walker: A Foundling's Christmas – ILN 25 December 1886.

The regime in Victorian times for those over the age of five was strict, as one would expect for the era. School lessons were interspersed with practical tasks – housework and needlework for the girls and gardening and handicraft for the boys – to support the institution and prepare the children for their lowly occupations as adults. The meals of boiled and roast beef or mutton, heavily padded out with bread and potatoes but, it seems, no other vegetables, were eaten in silence, and boys and girls were kept apart at all times. The early uniforms were made of drugget, but later replaced by brown serge edged in scarlet, and the girls wore white pinafores and bonnets. The children were undoubtedly institutionalised, and cut off from the outside world – except as specimens to be viewed by fashionable visitors supporting the Hospitals. However their lot was still preferable to being on the streets or enduring the humiliating regimes of contemporary workhouses.

One wonders what Christmas Day readers of the *ILN* thought of these 'charity' girls of the humblest origins having such dreams of being rescued by lovers from their humdrum lives. 'Humdrum' was what the Foundling Hospital was all about – cleanliness, obedience and basic vocational training, although not overt repression. The only exception was the training of some boys in musical instruments to form a band capable of public performances.

CHAPTER TEN

The World of Fairies, Sprites and Elves: Lands of Dangerous Enchantment

The Green Fairy Book

Although Victorian moralists thought many fairy tales were dangerously amoral and unwholesome reading for children, children themselves delighted in the strangeness of the environment, the magical creatures, the thrilling adventures, and the final satisfying triumph of good over evil. As printing costs got cheaper, more and more folk tales were published, and the moralists lost the battle to tie them to critical and corrective religious commentaries. In the latter part of the century several volumes of folk and fairy tales were gathered from across the world, and edited and published by Andrew Lang (1844-1912), a novelist and psychic researcher – although his wife and a team of assistants did much of the work. They were immensely popular, and on 26 November 1892 the *ILN* no doubt stimulated Christmas sales of his *The Green Fairy Book* with a two-page illustrated spread giving an enticing flavour of several of the stories. He had already published *The Folklore of France, The Blue Fairy Book, Perrault's Popular Tales* and *The Red Fairy Book,* and now there were a further 42 tales of spiteful and tyrannical kings, malevolent wizards and witches, and sinister shape-changing creatures acting in unsettling and bizarre ways, usually to test the courage and resolve of virtuous princesses who

Andrew Lang/Henry Justice Ford: Illustration from 'The Enchanted Snake' in The Green Fairy Book *– ILN 26 November 1892.*

were generally fortunate enough to find a sympathetic supernatural or human protector before the worst could happen. Lang's skilful illustrator, Henry Justice Ford (1860-1940), was adept in bringing to artistic life particularly threatening moments in the stories. For example, in *The Enchanted Snake* the fearful serpent who ingratiates himself with the royal family and seeks to marry the princess turns out to be a handsome prince – but only after numerous frights, extravagant spells, and the deaths of numerous birds and a fox to provide the blood necessary to rescue the badly wounded snake-prince from death.

What I Saw in the Fire

On 21 December 1861 the *ILN* published a striking and possibly disturbing montage of Christmas and comedic pantomime images drawn by Alfred Crowquill, the pseudonym of Alfred Henry Forrester (1804-72) (see overleaf). A nightmare effect is more than hinted in the title *What I Saw in the Fire*. Dancing flames, spiralling smoke and sooty patterns, it seems, have formed or suggested bizarre conjunctions out of his drifting thoughts of Christmases past, present and future.

When examined section by section there are a number of distinctive pantomime scenarios – groups of dancers, witches on broomsticks, anthropomorphic animals and figures with huge masks – but in the apparently chaotic picture each scenario is endowed with menace from its juxtaposition with other figures, usually of a totally different scale. It transferred the fantasies of contemporary pantomime to a completely new dimension and as it did so it blurred even further the distinction between comedy, tragedy and horror. Giant birds have overcome a bear, a rabbit faces a fox and vulture, small girls dance on the nose of a leering king, a tiny acrobat leaps into the mouth of a giant head, a bevy of witches descend upon a fairy godmother, another witch chases a frightened rider, and an ominous giant king looms over a happy young couple. In the midst of this surreal scene overflowing with menace the figure of Old Christmas looks quite content with everything around him.

Crowquill's own poem accompanies the illustration. It describes him dozing by the fire at Christmas:

When all at once amidst the glowing coal
I saw strange faces – stern, fantastic, droll;
Bright fairies, gnomes, and witches of the night;
Kings, ladies, sprites, all marshalled in the light;
Next frowning rocks, with castles on the top,
That blazed, and fumed, and spat, but did not stop
>*Crashing*
>*And dashing.*
Castles and people, and all the funny souls
Tumbled pell-mell amidst the burning coals.
>*Then strange*
>*The change!*
>*And the debris,*
>*You'd see*
Pick itself out of all the danger.
Turning at once to something, wilder, stranger.

With wry humour the poet says he envisages a new school of art emerging from his dream, but then is called to tea.

"I'll come", I said; then seized the poker straight,
And started all the phantoms from the grate,
Resolving just to try if mem'ry could
Produce the fantasy again on wood.
So, here it is; but really, on the whole,
The great idea was better in the coal.

The Enchanted Forest

In the 1891 Christmas Supplement *The Enchanted Forest* by Reginald Jones (1857-1920) featured two children who have wandered too near a cave being rescued from the imminent attack of lions by a fairy queen (see page 153). She has taken on the size of an adult human. Perhaps the snake slithering through the dark branches above her represents the ever-present threat of evil and danger faced by innocent children in the real world in the absence of protection and guidance as they grow up. As such the picture would have made an interesting Victorian conversation piece as a supernatural allegory of family life with its twists and turns, places of safety and danger, and variety of creatures posing threats or offering protection.

The rich historic clothing of the children suggests the illustration is a 'spin' on the story of *Babes in the Wood,* and despite the murderous intentions of their uncle these orphans are protected by supernatural beings and do not die in the forest as they did in the morbid traditional tale.

Alfred Crowquill: What I saw in the fire – ILN 21 December 1861.

Reginald Jones: The Enchanted Forest – ILN 1891 Christmas Supplement.

The Fairy Oak

The fearsome reputation and potentially fatal attractions of dark forests have informed folk-stories for centuries. No doubt the crooked shape of trees in the moonlight, rustling of leaves and branches, the cries of animals, and tales of people who wandered into forests and never reappeared all contributed to the belief in the trees themselves possessing a variety of protective spirits which may or may not be sympathetic to any humans wandering by.

The oak tree and oak grove were particularly important to the Celts. The oak grove was revered as a place of hospitality and safety, and the oak tree was a mystical symbol of bravery and truth. Other ancient connections may account for the word 'Druids' who were powerful pagan Celtic sages or priests but were also known across the pre-Roman and early Roman Mediterranean world. The Greek words 'drus' means tree and 'wid' means 'to know' from which 'Druid' might have evolved. The Sanskrit word for oak is 'Duir' which also means 'door' and suggests that the

William James Palmer: The Fairy Oak – ILN 1881 Christmas Supplement.

oak was seen as a sacred spiritual link with humanity. Oak trees had their own medicinal and magic properties. Their astringent bark was used to treat inflammation and wounds, and made into a tea it relieved dysentery. An oakwood fire kept illness away, and carrying an acorn kept one youthful and fertile.

The *ILN* reflected the Victorian fascination with folk-stories and magic, especially over Christmas, by publishing several seasonal illustrations in which oak trees and enchantment had central roles. *The Fairy Oak* engraved by William James Palmer (fl 1858-96) appeared in the 1881 Christmas Supplement and showed fairies dancing around an ancient oak tree as what appears to be a fairy army descends the hill behind a larger helmeted female warrior brandishing a staff. The shattered branch of the mighty tree symbolises the strength needed to endure and triumph over adversity. Here is another world living alongside humans, but sharing the spirit of the tree. In an accompanying poem by the theatre critic, playwright and lyricist Clement Scott (1841-1904) a grandfather tells his granddaughter that science would have us believe that fairies and enchantment do not exist, but says that our lives would be infinitely poorer if this was so. There would be no shiver of excitement, no leap of imagination, no stimulus for thought.

So, Sybil, believe in invisible caps,
In fountains that whisper, and flowers that weep,
In the loves of the fairyland court, for perhaps
You may glean for your comfort some mystical scraps
For thinking by day and for dreaming asleep.

Kate Greenaway: The Fairy Ring – ILN *28 December 1889.*

Breaking the The Fairy Ring

On 28 December 1889 a Kate Greenaway picture featured a young girl wandering alone in the forest who has just broken a fairy ring of mushrooms. The background is dark, and in a strange beam of light an ominous face much like Old Christmas can be seen on the bark of the oak tree behind her. The picture stands alone without a commentary, and readers were left to reflect on what was going on. Was she lost? Was she enchanted? Was she in danger? Folk tales did not help much, as some claimed entering the rings brought bad luck, even madness, while others said they were harbingers of good fortune and fertility.

By 1889 the nature of supernatural beings in contemporary stories was mellowing. More often than not they were sympathetic towards the predicament of humans, but still retained their love of mischief. Here the girl is utterly vulnerable as a result of her mistake, and at least one sprite is angry. However the girl has the natural ability, not granted to all human beings, to see the sprites, most of whom on closer inspection seem to be in good-spirits, and forgiveness is probably the order of the day.

In the 1880s Kate Greenaway was at the height of her fame as an illustrator, with young children and fairies as her speciality. 'Fairy rings' are naturally occurring circles of a wide variety of mushrooms found in forests and grassland.

Fairy Gifts

Fairy Gifts by John Anster Fitzgerald (1832-1906) appeared in the *ILN* on 19 December 1868. It is Christmas Eve, and a shaft of moonlight shines into the room. There are numerous winged creatures, some with youthful female forms and butterfly wings, but differentiated by various hair styles and adornments. Others are much smaller, with elfin features. What appears to be a bed post gives some idea of relative sizes, but possibly this is an attic rather than a main room as it is unclear whether the fairies are bringing presents to humans or, bearing in mind the ambiguity of relationships between the human and fairy world, taking human presents for themselves.

Fairies have a long history in Persian, Celtic, French and Germanic cultures. They were sometimes wingless and had to cling to birds to fly, but in most English representations they possessed delicate feminine beauty and the ability to fly and cast spells. Sometimes winged elves and sprites were included in the definition, not least because fairies could change their size and shapes. Goblins and other wingless beings were supernatural but definitely not fairies although they were often seen with them – but perhaps fairies could turn themselves into these less beautiful creatures. Interest in all of them soared in the Victorian era, and indeed into the twentieth century.

Fairies had to be treated with great caution as their relationship with humans was volatile, and they could as easily bring sickness and danger – and even the spiriting away of small children – as they could friendship and succour. Travellers by land or sea had be wary of fairies acting as will-o'-the-wisps or sirens seeking to entice them off their paths to danger. Fairies also wreaked vengeance of those who cut down their favourite tree, built on their hill, or desecrated their dell. Many folk stories said humans should always carry protective charms to ward off these superficially playful but deeply menacing beings. There were many theories about their origins. Were they a rival species or fallen angels or the spirits of the dead or the vital link between humans and the rest of the natural world?

The Romanticism of the late eighteenth and early nineteenth century proved fertile ground for the popularity of fairies, and folk-lore generally. They appeared in many literary works from those of William Blake (1757-1827), Sir Walter Scott (1771-1832) and James Hogg (aka the Ettick Shepherd, 1770-1835) to J.M. Barrie (1860-1937). And some very well known Victorian artists specialised in fairy paintings, not only John Anster Fitzgerald and Alfred Crowquill but also Daniel Maclise (1806-70), Richard Dadd (1817-86), Sir Joseph Noel Paton (1821-1901), Frederick Goodall (1822-1904), Richard Doyle (1824-83) and John Atkinson Grimshaw (1836-93). Clearly if the public liked such stories and paintings, writers and artists would continue to oblige – and diaphanously clad fairies became a common sight on canvas. Perhaps the popularity was to do with escaping the grimy urban landscape and the increasing hold of the clock on daily lives in factory and office, and to do with the stimulus to dream and soar beyond the 'now' to a world whose magical beings behaved very differently and were more closely attuned to the natural world. Maybe the Victorians were just enjoying themselves.

John Anster Fitzgerald: Fairy Gifts – ILN *19 December 1868.*

The Importance of Robins

John Anster Fitzgerald's fairy paintings included several touching on the old folk-poem *Who Killed Cock Robin?* One showed the robin held captive by fairies, another a robin defending his nest and a third fairies sleeping in his nest. An engraving of another work by him, *Poor Robin and the Fairies*, appeared in the *ILN*'s 1876 Christmas Supplement and featured a dead robin lying on what appears to be a water lily leaf with fairies in different garbs hovering sorrowfully over him (see overleaf). An accompanying poem by Edward Rose, best known as a playwright, (1849-1904) contains the verses:

I know beneath each frosted hedge,
 On every road, each icebound pond,
  Lies one of you past pain.

Nay, sometimes on my window-ledge
 A pretty bird I find, beyond
  My help so sad and vain!

O singers, that will sing no more!
 Dear poets, starved by cruel fate!
  Who knows, who weeps, your lot?
Are you, that gave us all your store,
 That loved us all, whom none could hate,
  By every soul forgot?

Ah, no! I think that in the night
 Come fairies, weeping bitterly,
  And o'er you scatter flowers!
So if to me came children bright
 And kissed, and wept, and mourned for me,
  How sweet were my last hours!

John Anster Fitzgerald: Poor Robin and the Fairies – ILN 1876 Christmas Supplement.

The robin has been killed by winter which in the poem *Who Killed Cock Robin?* is represented by the sparrow who admits to slaying him *with my bow and arrow.* Many other animals and birds then agree to make his shroud, dig his grave, read the service, carry the coffin, and ring the bell, and with the Victorian fascination with such anthropomorphic tales it was no wonder this poem was included in numerous illustrated story books. No-one seemed to have worried whether or not this murderous story without any obvious moral overtones was considered eminently suitable for children. Its origins are lost in the mists of time, but may refer to the killing of a much revered tribal or national leader.

The Victorians much preferred the traditions in which robins were harbingers of happiness and sources of comfort. Several stories said the red breast was gained when a robin sang to Jesus on the Cross and was pierced by the Crown of Thorns. Robins became messengers of comfort to humans, even at the peril of danger and death to the robins themselves. In the pantomime story of *Babes in the Wood*, which was popular in Victorian times, robins shelter and care for the children who

David Henry Friston: The Christmas Pantomimes (Robins sheltering the Babes in the Wood) – ILN 4 January 1873.

have fallen asleep – or, in some versions, died – after being deserted in the forest. In January 1873 the *ILN* printed a drawing by David Henry Friston (1820-1906) of such a scene in Drury Lane's pantomime. Robins were also closely associated with the red uniforms of Victorian postmen who not surprisingly were nicknamed 'robins', and numerous Christmas cards pictured the birds delivering greetings in the coldest weather. Their death in winter was therefore rendered particularly poignant.

Other old stories help explain the bizarre custom of Christmas images, including Christmas cards, featuring dead robins. As well as comforting the dying Jesus, a robin was believed to have ventured into Hell on behalf of humans to quench its fires with drops of water in its beak, and the red breast was the result of being badly scorched. Robins became the symbol of sacrifice as well as succour, and they were held to ease the journey into death, and from one life to another. To the Victorians a dead robin was a good omen – a true friend in life, and also after death. Indeed a robin would give his life for you. The sender of such a Christmas card was expressing similar devotion.

Death could be a frequent visitor to Victorian families, and perhaps such cards helped deal with its likely visitation – much like the elaborate death rituals with which the Victorians surrounded themselves, such the passing bell, viewing the body, photographing the dead person, elaborate mourning clothes, funeral processions, elaborate tombs, and lengthy periods of mourning.

A Christmas Dream

The Victorian relished dream paintings – those by Alfred Crowquill sold very well – and not surprisingly many paintings of fairies have a dream-like quality about them. On Boxing Day 1874 *A Christmas Dream* by Kate Greenaway showed a girl from a well-to-do family dressed ready to go out on a winter's day who had fallen asleep while waiting beside the fire. The accompanying text says she has had too many late nights over Christmas and *the material fabric of the brain lies just now at the mercy of a thronging multitude of remembered sensations, arousing the emotional nature to fantastic vagaries of appetite and conceits of external vision.* The Victorians thought many dreams emanated from over-eating, excessive activity and too much excitement. In *A Christmas Carol* the startled but defensive Ebenezer Scrooge initially declares of Jacob Marley's ghost, *You may be an undigested bit of beef, a blot of mustard, a crumb of cheese, a fragment of an underdone potato. There's more of gravy than a grave about you, whatever you are.*

In Greenaway's picture the girl dreams, apparently quite contentedly, about a host of mischievous imps upsetting the household decorum – playing with glass baubles, pulling threads from the carpet, pulling crackers, upsetting a flagon of wine, kicking a flying Christmas pudding, and lighting a match. One is giving another a ride on a walnut, a second is squeezing another in a nutcracker, a third is poking another by the fire with a toasting fork, and two others are about to disappear into a large pot. These imps are playful at one level, but selfishly do not care about each other and show no sign of caring for the girl. Perhaps the girl has had thoughts of breaking free from a strict and rather dull domestic regime, but *We know better,* asserted the commentary in a sly reference to darker interpretations of dreams, *and we can afford to disdain the licentious freaks of nature in sleep, which afford no sure indication of the moral disposition as it stands under the control of reason and conscience in waking hours.*

Kate Greenaway: A Christmas Dream *– ILN 26 December 1874.*

Toothpaste & Tea

By the 1880s supernatural beings were regularly invoked by manufacturers to help sell their wares, especially around Christmas. In December 1887 the Anglo-American Drug Company gave a pair of fairy wings to the hitherto wingless Flora, the Roman Goddess of Flowers, and surrounded her by winged cherubs to promote Floriline toothpaste. A verse in the advertisement draws cleverly upon the colourful fairy paintings and pantomime scenes of the time:

Fair Flora, the Goddess of Flowers, one day
Had summoned her legions around:
And thus she addressed them in sweet, mellow tones:
"My wishes let echo resound;
'Tis my word to distil from each beautiful flower,
That peeps from the dew-spangled scene,
The choicest, the sweetest, the richest of scents,
And such as are fit for a Queen.

Another advertiser drew upon the fashion for dream paintings. In early January 1890 the United Kingdom Tea Company of Mincing Lane, London, promoted its wares through a young woman dreaming that a host of sprites – mostly Chinese but interspersed with a few kilted Scots and tail-coated English merchants and clerks – were eager to have a pot of Oriental tea ready for her when she awoke.

Advertisement for United Kingdom Tea Company's Tea – ILN 11 January 1890.

Opposite: Advertisement for Floriline Toothpaste – ILN 3 December 1887.

The Perfumed Realms of Flora.

Fair Flora, the Goddess of Flowers, one day
  Had summoned her legions around ;
And thus she addressed them in sweet, mellow tones:
  "My wishes let echo resound ;
'Tis my wish to distil from each beautiful flower,
  That peeps from the dew-spangled scene,
The choicest, the sweetest, the richest of scents,
  And such as are fit for a Queen."

Then the beautiful rose raised its sweet-tinted head,
  And the violet crept from its bed ;
The jessamine, sweetbriar, lavender, too,
  Their fragrance around her now shed.
"Now list," said fair Flora ; and waving her hand,
  A change came around that fair scene :
For, bubbling aloft from a fountain of flowers,
  Came gushing the sweet "FLORILINE."

FLORILINE

FOR THE TEETH AND BREATH

Is the best Liquid Dentifrice.
Cleanses the Teeth,
Hardens the Gums,
And purifies the Breath.

Preserves the Teeth by
Removing parasites, and
Renders them pearly white.
Price 2s. 6d. per Bottle, in case.

Of all Chemists and Perfumers.

SOLE PROPRIETORS,
THE ANGLO-AMERICAN DRUG CO. (Limited),
33, FARRINGDON-ROAD, LONDON.

163

Bibliography

Barringer, T., *Men at Work: Art & Labour in Victorian Britain,* Yale/Paul Mellon Centre, 2005

Briggs, A., *Victorian People,* Odhams, 1954

Briggs, A., *Victorian Cities,* Odhams, 1963

Briggs, A., *Victorian Things,* Batsford, 1988

Cannadine, D., *Victorious Century: The United Kingdom 1800-1906,* Penguin, 2017

Caputo, J.D., *Deconstruction in a Nutshell: A Conversation with Jacques Derrida,* Fordham UP, Revised Edition 2020

Chadwick, O., *The Victorian Church: Part One 1829-1859,* SCM , 1966

Chadwick, O., *The Victorian Church: Part Two 1860-1901,* SCM, 1982

Flanders, J., *The Victorian House: Domestic Life from Childhood to Deathbed,* Harper, 2004

Flanders, J., *Consuming Passions: Leisure & Life in Victorian Britain,* Harper, 2007

Flanders, J., *The Victorian City: Everyday Life in Dickens' London,* Arrow, 2012

Flanders, J., *Christmas: A History,* Picador, 2018

Graham-Dixon, A., *A History of British Art,* BBC, 1996

Heffer, S., *High Minds: The Victorians and the Birth of Modern Britain,* Windmill, 2014

Lang, A., (Ed), *The Green Fairy Book,* Dover Reprint, 1965

Marsden, G. (Ed), *Victorian Values: Personalities & Perspectives in Nineteenth Century Society,* Longman, 1990

Nead, L., *Myths of Sexuality: Representations of Women in Victorian Britain,* Wiley/Blackwell, 1990

Nead, L., *Victorian Babylon: People, Streets & Images in Nineteenth Century London,* Yale UP, 2005

Picard, L., *Victorian London: The Life of a City 1840-1870,* Phoenix, 2005

Thomas, J., *Victorian Narrative Painting,* Tate Publishing, 2000

Thompson, F.M.L., *The Rise of Respectable Society: A Social History of Victorian Britain 1830-1900,* Fontana, 1988

Vicinus, M., *A Widening Sphere: Changing Roles of Victorian Women,* Routledge, 1980

Wilson, A.N., *The Victorians,* Arrow, 2003

Wood, C., *The Pre-Raphaelites,* Weidenfeld & Nicolson, 1981

Wood, C., *Paradise Lost: Paintings of English Country Life & Landscape 1850-1914,* Grange, 1993

Wood, C., *Victorian Paintings,* Weidenfeld & Nicolson, 1999

Websites

https://victorianweb.org *The Victorian Web: Literature, History & Culture in the Age of Victoria* – notably for articles relating to Artists, the 'Gentleman', London Theatres and Pantomime, Needlewomen, Dressmakers & Milliners, Newspapers and Periodicals, Philanthropy, Ragged Schools, Religious Beliefs and Doubts, Slums and Slumming, Social Class, and Women – Class and Occupations.

jamesalder.co.uk. Biographies of artists

Index